D0354369

LIFE IN LIFE

Liya Openhearts save souls Be Brave I love you

LIFE IN LIFE

*Live Longer, Strengthen
Your Relationships, and
Create a Healthier Life:
A Meditation Journal*

Dr. Laurie Ann Levin

BENBELLA

BENBELLA BOOKS, INC. • DALLAS, TX

Copyright © 2015 by Laurie Ann Levin

All rights reserved. No part of this book may be used or reproduced in any manner whatsoever without written permission, except in the case of brief quotations embodied in critical articles or reviews.

Trademark: Life in Life™ and the related trade dress are trademarks of Dr. Laurie A. Levin and/or her affiliates in the United States and other countries, and may not be used without written permission.

Information Disclaimer: The information provided in this publication is not a substitute for professional psychological advice and care. If you have specific needs, please see a professional healthcare provider. Dr. Laurie Ann Levin assumes no responsibility for outcomes resulting from the use of information contained in this publication. Dr. Levin expressly disclaims (denies or renounces) all liability for injury or damages arising out of use of, reference to, or reliance on such information.

BENBELLA

BenBella Books, Inc.
10300 N. Central Expressway
Suite #530
Dallas, TX 75231
www.benbellabooks.com
Send feedback to feedback@benbellabooks.com

Printed in the United States of America
10 9 8 7 6 5 4 3 2 1

Library of Congress Cataloging-in-Publication Data
Levin, Laurie Ann, 1953-
   Life in life : how earth riders become light workers / Dr. Laurie Ann Levin.
      pages cm
   Includes bibliographical references and index.
      ISBN 978-1-941631-06-5 (hardback) — ISBN 978-1-941631-07-2 (electronic) 1. Meditation. 2. Spiritual life. I. Title.
   BL627.L485 2015
   158.1'2—dc23

                                                                                          2015022835

Editing by Erin Kelley
Copyediting by Oriana Leckert
Proofreading by Greg Teague and Cape Cod Compositors, Inc.
Author photo by Alberto Romeu Photography
Front cover design by Connie Gabbert
Full cover design by Sarah Dombrowsky
Text design and composition by John Reinhardt Book Design
Printed by Lake Book Manufacturing

Distributed by Perseus Distribution
perseusdistribution.com

To place orders through Perseus Distribution:
Tel: (800) 343-4499
Fax: (800) 351-5073
E-mail: orderentry@perseusbooks.com

Significant discounts for bulk sales are available.
Please contact Glenn Yeffeth at glenn@benbellabooks.com or (214) 750-3628.

This book is dedicated to my Jerry.
I love you with all my soul, all my heart, and all my might.
Forever, always, and beyond, may we inspire the perpetual kiss between heaven and earth.

To my Beloved Three Sirens of Song:
Jane, Cathy, and Dorothy.
Thank you for all your love and light.

Contents

Part 2: THE BURNING BUSH   91

Miraculous Energy, Sacred Light, Purity, Clarity, Love

Part 3: THE TREE OF LIFE   177

Unity

PREFACE

THIS MEDITATION JOURNAL is all about your personal pursuit of happiness and fulfillment, and learning how to give yourself the gift of love and light. Often the phrase "love and light" is glossed over simply as an obligatory signature line or salutation, but I believe it is the adoption of love and light that supplies the consciousness with goodness itself, the very bedrock of refinement and healing, helping you overtake any trauma and anxiety in your life.

Your capacity to heal is commensurate with your ability to let in the light.

Undefended and open love can usher in that exquisite orchestration of order and trust in a lifetime otherwise corrupted by dysfunction. Ritualized invitation for access and reception of the highest qualities of the supreme genius of love and light reinforce a resourcing in personal expansion beyond what we have previously fathomed as linear reality. Love and light are each both a noun and a verb, enabling giving and receiving, aspiring and being at peace, loving self and others at the same time.

It does not matter if you have never meditated or if you actually meditate your way through life, nor does it matter what your belief system is or whether you are spiritual or a non-believer; this bedside book's call to self-discovery will take you on a reconnaissance toward your most expansive consciousness. Whether master or beginner, whether alone, with the intimacy of a partner, or in a group, all is on track for you and everyone to access your heart's desire with the exercises in this book.

Everyone's approach to meditation is unique, and you will have your own relationship with your vastness. Your meditations must be comfortable—you may feel the need to move or sit or even lie very still, you may feel more comfortable with your eyes open or closed, and you may be more or less comfortable with enhancements of music, ocean sounds, fragrance, water elements, candlelight, or near darkness.

As a personal journal, your own automatic writings are prompted by parables and meditative prayers that are universal and inclusive of all religions, philosophies, and belief systems. This invitation to call on your own self-illumination is also predicated on the physics of neuroscience. Through the sheer act of meditation, new pathways are established in your brain and there is a physical rewiring as the brain reshapes itself. With instructive meditation, you can increase your intuitive reception, regulate your fear center, and enhance your ability to concentrate, focus, and make effective decisions. You are at the helm.

In addition, the secure practice of meditation and automatic writing creates a safe place, a sanctuary to experience sensations beyond the five senses. In that safe place, there is room to break through your psychological, emotional, and spiritual barriers, leading to an understanding of the "positive system" that provides solid grounding and expansion, no matter what you might be struggling with. Love and light eventually take on new meaning, as they become the staple ingredients for your evolution and growth.

Life in Life is not only the *life* you lead, but also the *life* "with*in*" your life: meditation that regularly employs the consciousness of goodness, truth, and beauty, guiding you toward your distinctive expansion.

Life in Life is a meditation journal designed for you to reach the part of yourself that is connected to that "extra" consciousness of goodness. From that pivotal connection, your most expanded self, outside of old patterns, can nestle in an internal sense of wellbeing, help refine your life's purpose, improve overall health and wellness, alter neural pathways to ameliorate trauma cycles, unleash your innate intuition, and sharpen problem-solving and executive functioning, all together in the harmony of a happier life.

We all need regular and emergency meditation to dilute the usual reflex of resistance, that negative push backward away from the momentum toward the light. With *Life in Life*, you will reconfigure each moment to bring everything required for light and love to prevail and endure.

Stay open for the light, for your own Highest Self devoid of looping or repetitive negative behaviors; be supple and full of love, and all will fall into place with comfort, completion, and ease.

HOW TO BEGIN

- While in the beginning stages of the book, read the whole chapter out loud, including the exercises, before you start. The reading aloud will help put into your physical world the energies, clarity, and sharing you are embarking upon.
- Read all prompts to each chapter and exercise (even if you may not feel you are a Master, or are actually working with a partner), as the suggestion boxes may reveal important information for you.
- After all has been read out loud, and meditation parables have been pondered, read the exercise suggestions again and then begin writing.
- Use either pen or pencil to write in your book. You can supplement your journal with more paper, or dictate your journal

entries in the "notes" section of an electronic device. However you do it, keep a running journal for review. You will better see the arc of your expansion and see which moments have echoes through your life.

- Your week's chapter may be taken out of order or revisited for deeper understanding. This is a living book that is in constant co-creation with your evolution and expansion. As you grow, you will often see newer, deeper meaning from just living in opened awareness.

- Self-exploration is a gift; above all, receive the joy from the discovery. Enjoy it with intimates you trust, and try to witness each other's lives and laugh together when clarity is apparent.

YOU are Life in Life. To paraphrase George Bernard Shaw: "We don't grow old, we become old by not growing."

Induction to Meditation

FIND A QUIET, sacred place where you most likely will not be interrupted. If you prefer, ask a friend or partner or cherished group to do this with you.

If your location is not sacred to you, perform a ritual or ceremony to infuse the surroundings with love and light (light candles, say prayers, call on that which is holy to you).

Slow your breath, close your eyes, and, through guided imagery, conjure a virtual experience of being bathed in white light. Perhaps the light surrounds you as you walk into it, or perhaps the light shines from within your body. Do it in whatever way is most calming to your senses.

If you walk into your white light, maybe you will look up at the sun, or feel the moonlight shining on your skin, and disintegrate your dense body into the consciousness of the ALL, blurring the borders of your body into the state of LOVE. Imagine yourself wherever would be the most peaceful and calming to you.

Call on your Highest Self, or whatever is most holy to you, to begin a dialogue with yourself. Invite in all that previously supported you—your thought patterns, beliefs, emotions, and body structures—for expansion. Reassure yourself that expansion never eliminates what you already are. We want to honor all that you are and have been. You are simply inviting in the expanded highest consciousness of YOU to assist you.

Perhaps imagine the orchestra of YOU warming up before a concert. Slowly see more and more instruments being added—percussion, strings, horns.

Gently remind yourself and your being that in this expansion YOU WILL NEVER UN-KNOW WHAT YOU ALREADY KNOW.

Feel, say, and know, "I am love," and "I am perfect in every way." Allow yourself to be loved and feel loved through this exercise. If at any time feelings of discord come over you, review the reasons. Take notes. These tangles are precious. Try to untangle. Please do not be hard on yourself. All will be illuminated in its perfect timing. Trust and start again.

Part 1

THE TREE OF AWAKENING
Attaining Supreme Enlightenment

Women as the Initiators of Life

WOMEN OF THE WORLD are about to battle with all the strife (both personal and global) and make a clear decision to exhaust their need and the world's requirement for mess. "Women" does not just refer to females, but to the feminine energy of men as well. Now is the time we have exhausted our need for pain, deficit, chaos, confusion, and fear. We can have an experience of completion with ease. What was prescribed, rehearsed, imprinted, or locked away can now be encouraged.

This will result in a great healing, of a greater proportion than ever realized. We will declare a state of LOVE. ALL will be in revelation. Unsettled happenings will be illuminated soon as mere occurrence. We might uproot all living understandings of life, in seeing each and every one as eternal.

This realization will bring in the New Worlds. ALL will be ONE.

EXERCISE 1: EXHAUSTING OLD PATTERNS

Below is the preparation meditation that will repeat at the top of each exercise in small font so that you may refresh yourself each time you meditate. Additional steps and suggestions may be added, so please read each meditation as you need it. Feel free to customize your meditation for your comfort. Some people need to be still, some need to move, sway, sing, chant, wave their arms in the air, or put their feet in soil. Some will enjoy visual, olfactory, or auditory enhancements. Pay attention to the inductions that work best for your style. Take note when change is necessary. Feel free to mix it up: You might need to change when the style you choose becomes stale, requires enormous unsettling effort, or becomes distracting. Please experiment, though, as the style that seems most challenging may in fact be one that eventually works best. You are trying to break free of old patterns, so enjoy!

If you are doing these exercises with a friend, partner, or group, set ground rules for the sanctity of the intimacy and the sharing. Meditate together to discover what everyone's goals are, both as a group and as individuals. Make certain that ALL are in agreement before moving forward. If trust issues arise, listen to the vulnerabilities of each person and decide together how to love each other through feelings and occurrences. Group work or partner work may be arduous and rewarding, as you are exploring your expansion with another as they explore with you. That is a treasured gift of enormous proportion and must be valued as such.

Induction to Meditation

Please see page xvii.

Personalize Your Practice

BEGINNER — Just showing up, reading the words, and sitting in the openness of receiving is everything. It is an invitation to your self that you are now ready for your expansion. Let the place and time of your meditation be special to you, so as to luxuriate, even if just for a moment. Whether words come or not, this book is your journey. If you operate concretely, then write your goals, but try to connect energetically, appreciate your senses, and blur your body into the sensations as you imagine the white light. If you fall asleep, all is perfect. Trust and enjoy.

MASTER — Most of us have areas where we feel up against the walls of our patterns. We may loop, perseverate, or unintentionally reignite old trauma. The orchestra is a metaphor. The visualization of adding more instruments is a beginning to invite back all parts of you, much like a soul retrieval, as well as inviting more expansive energies for your Highest Good to illuminate. You are ready to operate from the full expression of a very vast you.

PARTNER — The delicate compassion and loving acceptance can be set up when prayer begins the circle of sharing. Set the mood, the conditions, and the honoring with attention to each person's needs. Let each share without inter-ruption. Try to find support in your heart for your partner's worth to you, as it might be a direct reflection of your compassion toward your self. Be circum-spect about whom you invite in as a group member, as it is very difficult to shift members midstream. At the same time, trust in all events as fodder for growth. Stay open and caring to your self and to others at the same time.

Begin your sacred journal handwritten or digitally—whatever is most comfortable for you. Write at the top of the page, each and every time, or use the space in this book:

DATE _____

PLACE _____

TIME _____

WHAT IS MINE TO DO?

Ask the expansive part of yourself.

_____

_____

_____

_____

_____

WHAT IS MINE TO KNOW OR UNDERSTAND THAT I WOULDN'T EVEN KNOW TO ASK?

You are asking your Highest Self to be open to that which you may never have imagined. You are asking to see beyond your customary beliefs, ideas, and construction. Leave room for the possibility of receiving answers in both conventional and unconventional ways.

_____

_____

_____

_____

_____

HOW CAN I LOVE MYSELF BEST RIGHT NOW?

As if you are listening to a friend, stay empty, feel, see, hear, and know. If it's more comfortable, close your eyes to receive. Then write whatever comes to you—with no judgment or editing. If you are visual and images come, write what you see. If you hear an internal voice, small or large, write what you hear. If you have thoughts, body sensations, or emotional knowing, take notes. You are chronicling your expansion, a wondrous, winding road, a treasure that is all yours.

2

Love of Self and Other at the Same Time

THERE ARE REASONS to come together without competition and in the name of a larger network of loving regard. Life is renewed because we are ready to have a life of living together as one. We call on each other and live a fuller existence, reaping the benefits of one another's knowledge and assistance.

Now the time has come when we want to find a new path. Love all, all the ways you love. Do not hesitate to reach further than others have discussed before. Be of grace. Go forward and reach for the unfathomable.

You have a gift to give. Go forward to hear the way to a sense of protection together.

EXERCISE 2: WORLDS COME TOGETHER

Call on your Highest Self, or whatever is most holy to you, to begin a dialogue with yourself. Invite your Highest Self to love yourself and others at the same time.

Just saying those simple words—*love of self and other at the same time*—will open up visuals and feelings. Envision holding hands with many others and start to see worlds come together, for the ALL is one. Assure yourself that these guided imageries and exercises are always of highest love and light.

If uncomfortable or resistant feelings, visions, or experiences come over you, lovingly remind your Highest Self that in some way this is a new beginning. This may threaten the very fabric of what you originally birthed yourself here to participate in, but you are now ready to co-create a new self, ready to experience your expansion to include love of self and other at the same time.

Listen without your ears, see without your eyes, and begin new intuitive receiving. Stay empty as you invite it all in. Begin automatic writing: a stream of unedited thoughts, feelings, or emotions. When finished, review what you wrote and save for a later date. Keep all your writings in order, as you may decide to repeat this at another date to compare.

Induction to Meditation

Please see page xvii.

Personalize Your Practice

BEGINNER – Trust in letting the gift of support in. Try not to be concerned with exactly who or how, but know that many signals of assistance can be made clear through synchronicities and surprises. This work will introduce you to new ways of deciphering yourself and your body.

If you start to cough, twitch, forget where you are, or react in ways that are bothersome, be kind to yourself. New perspectives toward your body language will start to make sense.

Intuitive material comes in many ways. Take a second and ask yourself if there was something you were able to see without your eyes or hear without your ears. This new focus on receiving/listening is somewhat like flexing a new muscle, or you may have been doing it your whole life, but never thought about it as a process or something outside of yourself. Watch, hear, and feel with a heightened sensitivity. No longer take

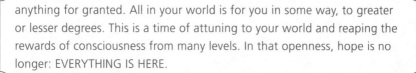

anything for granted. All in your world is for you in some way, to greater or lesser degrees. This is a time of attuning to your world and reaping the rewards of consciousness from many levels. In that openness, hope is no longer: EVERYTHING IS HERE.

MASTER – We cannot reach expansion with the same methodology that created our constraint. We are calling on assistance that is bigger than our own construction, while making very certain that the assistance is only of the highest qualities of love and light. That deters peripheral consciousness, not of our wanting, to abide our metaphysical demands for our greatest good.

These exercises are evergreen, and you can read your responses as well as the requests that inspire the answers over and over. Each time is a new moment. Trust that the moment will bring all.

If you are used to meditation where you clear your mind, or have prayers that are structured, ask for guidance in a new way. Even if you do not know what to ask, trust that you are now a vessel readied for revelation.

PARTNERS – Compassion to another's inward reflection may be a much-needed discovery of self. Each member will describe their experience differently. Treat all experience as worthy, with no judgment, as one might talk about a negative ion to a positive ion. They both serve a purpose in a relationship, but one is not evil or good.

Some members may have unique ways to explore their inner worlds. Please find the openness of heart to listen. If you find yourself triggered by any of the material, support and grow from your reactivity. The gift of your partnership may actually be to see where you get charged.

Meditation is the very antidote to reactivity. When someone goes through a traumatic experience, their brain responds in fight, flight, or freeze. There is an override of our frontal cortex. Meditation recalibrates the cross-hemispheric communication, and you begin to smooth through new ways to view or perceive and let go of past issues.

Compassion toward others instills compassion toward self, and vice versa.

DATE _____

PLACE _____

TIME _____

WHAT IS MINE TO DO?

Ask the expansive part of yourself.

_____

_____

_____

_____

WHAT IS MINE TO KNOW OR UNDERSTAND THAT I WOULDN'T EVEN KNOW TO ASK?

You are asking your Highest Self to be open to that which you may never have imagined. You are asking to see beyond your customary beliefs, ideas, and construction. Leave room for the possibility of receiving answers in both conventional and unconventional ways.

_____

_____

_____

_____

_____

HOW CAN I LOVE MYSELF BEST RIGHT NOW?

As if you are listening to a friend, stay empty, feel, see, hear, know. If it's more comfortable, close your eyes to receive. Then write whatever comes to you—with no judgment or editing. If you are visual and images come, write what you see. If you hear an internal voice, small or large, write what you hear. If you have thoughts, body sensations, or emotional knowing, take notes. You are chronicling your expansion, a wondrous, winding road, a treasure that is all yours.

3

I Am a Truly Powerful and Free Person

YOU HAVE LIVED out completion for everyone in your immediate family, meaning that you have fulfilled agreements for growth and karmic debt.

Now it is time for us all to work together as the family of man. You consult your own loving consciousness and go in to listen to your heart. It is there that you receive counsel.

Through that act, you alter and elevate the ALL.

EXERCISE 3: I AM ONE WITH EVERYTHING

Dear Highest Self,
  What were my previous commitments to:

1. Myself – [list each]

2. Loved ones – [list each]

3. How have I fulfilled these commitments?

_____

4. What might my new, expanded commitment be that I may not even know?

_____

This exercise may take many sittings. Review and review. Make sure you feel comfortable with the answers from your Highest Self.

Then repeat the exercise from the vantage point of the Highest Self of all those participating in your list. Whether they are alive or deceased, imagine yourself walking into their being. Ask their Highest Self, on the etheric plane, to come and dialogue with you.

There is no need to call on them in real time. This is an exercise of bilocation, where your physical body is in one location, but your etheric body visits and communes with the consciousness of love and light that is here for your highest good.

Take notes through automatic writing. There is no need for editing. Meditate on your answers and compare them for alignment and fulfillment to each other, even if you never lived out your agreement in Earth life terms together. (This could apply, for example, to the biological mother of an adopted child, a deceased family member, etc.)

Begin automatic writing; when finished, review what you wrote and save for a later date. Keep all your writings in order.

Induction to Meditation

Please see page xvii.

Personalize Your Practice

BEGINNER – Attempt to find the open, loving heart space to join with an other. It is a supposition, a projection, and a wondering from your most generous self. Bilocation is a sophisticated metaphysical joining with your self and their Highest Self. Prepare the entry to an other with only the highest qualities of Love and Light. Bilocation means simultaneously being in two places at the same time. You can be within your own physical body while receiving consciousness, visuals, and information from that which is not physically with you. You are knowingly activating, inviting, or requesting such information.

   If you feel any restraint, try at another time as it should be a free feeling. At its foundation, this is simply a lesson in compassion.

MASTER – Bilocation cannot be done with a soul that is not in reciprocation. If you are having any pushback, try using an intermediary that is in alignment with your belief system, such as God, Buddha, consciousness, Creator, Allah, Ganesh, and so on to be an emissary on your behalf. Check with the emissary to inquire about timing, receptivity, and the preferred line of questioning.

   Learn from obstacles, which can be effective information toward your own expansion. See if the pushback is but a reflection of a needed view of your own internal pushback. Keep untangling through using your self and your internal landscape before going to an other as the reason for resistance. When you have cleaned up your resistance, you will be better equipped to inquire from an other.

PARTNER – If there's time in your group meeting, try "going in" on each other, as an exercise. Quiet and energy-clearing is necessary before you begin.

   Share lovingly with an open mind. Some will be easier to read than others, and some may not be ready, either consciously or unconsciously, to see what is revealed. If intuitive material gleaned doesn't size up in any way to the other, know that you may have been picking up information from an outside source.

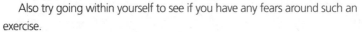

Also try going within yourself to see if you have any fears around such an exercise.

Make a conscious prayer to utilize your Highest Self to reach their Highest Self.

DATE _____

PLACE _____

TIME _____

WHAT IS MINE TO DO?

Ask the expansive part of yourself.

_____

_____

_____

_____

WHAT IS MINE TO KNOW OR UNDERSTAND THAT I WOULDN'T EVEN KNOW TO ASK?

You are asking your Highest Self to be open to that which you may never have imagined. You are asking to see beyond your customary beliefs, ideas, and construction. Leave room for the possibility of receiving answers in both conventional and unconventional ways.

_____

_____

_____

HOW CAN I LOVE MYSELF BEST RIGHT NOW?

As if you are listening to a friend, stay empty, feel, see, hear, know. If it's more comfortable, close your eyes to receive. Then write whatever comes to you—with no judgment or editing. If you are visual and images come, write what you see. If you hear an internal voice , small or large, write what you hear. If you have thoughts, body sensations, or emotional knowing, take notes. You are chronicling your expansion, a wondrous, winding road, a treasure, and that is yours.

4

Why Journal?

WHEN YOU WRITE, you consecrate the changes received. You know that meetings have taken place to chronicle and express your work. You have joined in to an etheric moment that will be realized when you physically bring the newly revised commitments through.

Just know that we are all together. When you type, write longhand, or dictate, you bring the voice of all our worlds. That is why your Highest Self's voice flows freely and clearly. Sometimes it is not of you or your style. We, the All, love you. You have worked very hard to be a conduit, a messenger of the Divine, a counselor and a healer to a new world view.

All is right with the world; watch it unfold.

EXERCISE 4: EASE AND COMPLETION

Who helps me write from my Highest Self? Are there voices that harmonize to help me find my highest voice?

How might I help you, give gratitude to you, work with you? ("You" = guidance, divine assistance, etc.)

Induction to Meditation

Please see page xvii.

Personalize Your Practice

BEGINNER – Try not to be too linear or concrete in thinking about who might be your "guidance." When asking, open your mind to what feels good, possible, and potentially there for you.

MASTER – The physical act of writing brings the spiritual commitment into the dense world as an action. Enjoy the manifestation of your dreams to eventual realities through the process of writing.

PARTNERS – Share your writings with sanctity, honoring and graciousness. No matter how different your words and style and process might be from others', please see the beauty in each to each.

DATE _____

PLACE _____

TIME _____

WHAT IS MINE TO DO?

Ask the expansive part of yourself.

_____

_____

_____

_____

_____

_____

WHAT IS MINE TO KNOW OR UNDERSTAND THAT I WOULDN'T EVEN KNOW TO ASK?

You are asking your Highest Self to be open to that which you may never have imagined. You are asking to see beyond your customary beliefs, ideas, and construction. Leave room for the possibility of receiving answers in both conventional and unconventional ways.

_____

_____

_____

_____

_____

_____

_____

HOW CAN I LOVE MYSELF BEST RIGHT NOW?

As if you are listening to a friend, stay empty, feel, see, hear, and know. If it's more comfortable, close your eyes to receive. Then write whatever comes to you—with no judgment or editing. If you are visual and images come, write what you see. If you hear an internal voice, small or large, write what you hear. If you have thoughts, body sensations, or emotional knowing, take notes. You are chronicling your expansion, a wondrous winding road, a treasure that is all yours.

5

Warrant for Your Arrest

WE ARE ALL gathered together to see the dawning of a new time when all can live in peace and light. Total illumination will be the harbinger for the beginning of a new time of total repose and relief.

Please understand that your quest for understanding life will effortlessly lead the way to the new dawn. You are the relief that we have all been waiting for, even if you wrestle with your place and all is not revealed so quickly.

EXERCISE 5: PLANTING THE SEEDS

What are my new commitments, co-created with all that is holy to me?

How might I be of, in, and for my highest purpose?

After writing about commitments and purpose, now, through prayer, invite all loved ones in to support your new expanded direction. If you feel the urge to write or artistically represent an invitation, enjoy that process as well. It is for you. If you care to share, please meditate first and consult your heart as to the best and most appropriate methods for extending. What is most significant about this exercise for many will be the support you are inviting in ON YOUR NEW TERMS.

Induction to Meditation

Please see page xvii.

Personalize Your Practice

BEGINNER – You are "arresting" current ineffective behaviors and commitments, walking through a threshold from old you to new you.

Perhaps there are family members, colleagues, or an intimate mate who may not consciously support your newly declared and now found purpose. Do not worry. Simply request and invite, in your self-guided automatic writing, that they support you. You are engaging your Highest Self to your new expansive purpose.

See what unfolds over time; as you are shifting, allow time for them to shift. As you become more committed to your expansion, they will respond consciously or unconsciously. Watch. Record. Reflect. All information allows for your clarity with successive steps forward.

MASTER – When one comes to the end of their construction, they often feel like they want to die. Death is the death of the old.

New commitments made from a more expansive stance are required.

In taking on even more expansion than previously committed to before, please demand that which is here for your Highest Good to come. It may not appear to you in a linear fashion, as a hologram might have the entire picture all at once. It may come as animal/totem guidance symbolizing strengths and protections, or as a sneak preview of potential expression.

Whichever way it shows itself, stay open to the idea that the information may be beyond that which has come before, that you are ready to discover new alternatives and commitments to yourself at a soul level. You are now recreating, not just accepting and allowing.

PARTNER – Perhaps ask at a soul level: What are the commitments you each have to the others in the group? It is possible, before ever meeting, that you agreed, at a soul level, to fulfill something bigger than you imagined or believed on a linear, time/space earth level.

It is possible that you or they may understand material beyond their own understanding of self. Be gentle in sharing your wisdom and subtle in your conviction.

Also, body pangs, twitches, goosebumps, and wafts of visual daydream-like images may appear in the group. You might be picking up intuitive material from one in the group. The fact that it came to *you* is significant. Try to decipher origin and meaning lovingly to self and others.

There can be consciousness that once was a living being that is attached to a person in the group, or attached to the location you are holding the meeting. Please sweep the surrounds and participants. Only consciousness and energies of the highest qualities of love and light are invited. Ask all else to go immediately. Wait a bit and feel the difference. Enjoy the elevated connection with no interference or static.

DATE _____

PLACE _____

TIME _____

WHAT IS MINE TO DO?

Ask the expansive part of yourself.

_____

_____

_____

_____

_____

WHAT IS MINE TO KNOW OR UNDERSTAND THAT I WOULDN'T EVEN KNOW TO ASK?

You are asking your Highest Self to be open to that which you may never have imagined. You are asking to see beyond your customary beliefs, ideas, and construction. Leave room for the possibility of receiving answers in both conventional and unconventional ways.

_____

_____

_____

_____

_____

HOW CAN I LOVE MYSELF BEST RIGHT NOW?

As if you are listening to a friend, stay empty, feel, see, hear, know. If it's more comfortable, close your eyes to receive. Then write whatever comes to you—with no judgment or editing. If you are visual and images come, write what you see. If you hear an internal voice, small or large, write what you hear. If you have thoughts, body sensations, or emotional knowing, take notes. You are chronicling your expansion, a wondrous winding road, a treasure that is all yours.

6

Earth Rider as a Light Worker

PERHAPS YOU FOUND your newly expanded purpose includes service, love, or healing? Please invite in the possibility to include a future mission or purpose as a conduit of expansion beyond location, direction, and outside conventional time, so as to elevate beyond the Three Dimensions. Enjoy being a light worker in whatever expression you are in.

EXERCISE 6: BEYOND THE THREE DIMENSIONS

What might I need to know, that I would not even know to ask, about my possible participation as a conduit of expansion?

Begin your automatic writing. Review. Does what you received include a future mission and/or purpose as a conduit of expansion beyond location, direction, and outside conventional time, so as to elevate beyond the Three Dimensions?

If not, please inquire as to how or why. You may have a commitment to be more grounded, practical, or skeptical in your expression. Ask about the nature of your expression. Everyone has different specialties.

Remember: if at any time negative or resistant feelings or thoughts wash over you, write and ask for more understanding. Keep pursuing understanding, knowing that you are expanding from customary and previous expression. Comfort yourself and repeat the top of the exercise. Begin again. Be gentle and loving. All information is valid.

Induction to Meditation

Please see page xvii.

Personalize Your Practice

BEGINNER – Your purpose and mission is often not the same as how you define your work. It is a loftier soul expression of that which fuels you or is about to fuel you.

A Light Worker is one who spreads light. It can be as simple as sharing your smile, giving a heartfelt compliment, exchanging joy-filled eye contact. Just being you spreads light.

Now imagine how you might spread light beyond the constraints of time and space. Possibly when you think of someone fondly, or pray for someone's health, you are sending energetic light beyond time and space. You are a channel, a conduit for healing. You may say or do the exact right thing for someone in need. Even if you don't receive corroboration right away, trust that once you commit to serving the light you will get feedback from your world and the people and animals in it. Declare to your self, "I am a receiver and giver of light." Let it all unfold.

MASTER – This is beyond words, to walk into your vastness and expand yourself to be Divine. Every step you take, wherever you are, you are a pump of giving and receiving light. Living in a conscious, prayerful, care-full way, paying attention to all the realms beyond the five senses, is a rich life.

(Continued)

Imagine spreading your light to all realms of you and your timelessness; as your ancestors are in your DNA, so too is your future. Give to yourself the gift of being a plurality with the Divine.

If you cry, or are filled with pools of extra electricity, or have sensations you may not have had before, sometimes complimentary, anonymous, and generous consciousness might be within you. Often it is with a message, and sometimes the energetic support is message enough. Take a pause and inquire. Close your eyes and ask that which is here for your Highest Good to speak to you.

If you encounter any resistances, imagine walls of protection or defenses coming down. As we are all one, we are no longer in need of defenses as we knew them to be. Please assure yourself and feel into what trust feels like. In a second you could erect those walls again, but we are going universal, living in every slice of time at all times. In feeling the Oneness is a sense of well-being and trust.

PARTNER – In the search for meaning, we might find that there is usually mutuality in any exchange. The agreement to work together serves all of you.

In opening yourself up to your partner as well as the unseen energies that come to assist, you can trust that you most likely will not be overwhelmed through too much information.

There are rules of the universe that what's meant for you will only be for you. Yes, there is randomness, but it is not often. Through systematic questioning with your Highest Self, your elevated and expansive self, inquire within what is the mutuality of each exchange.

Everybody has their own entry to the quality of their perception, clarity, and reception of information.

See each in the group as a potential piece of self to learn from and through. Share fearlessly any and all resistances, because your resistances become grist for the mill for everyone.

DATE _____

PLACE _____

TIME _____

WHAT IS MINE TO DO?

Ask the expansive part of yourself.

_____

_____

_____

_____

WHAT IS MINE TO KNOW OR UNDERSTAND THAT I WOULDN'T EVEN KNOW TO ASK?

You are asking your Highest Self to be open to that which you may never have imagined. You are asking to see beyond your customary beliefs, ideas, and construction. Leave room for the possibility of receiving answers in both conventional and unconventional ways.

_____

_____

_____

_____

_____

HOW CAN I LOVE MYSELF BEST RIGHT NOW?

As if you are listening to a friend, stay empty, feel, see, hear, know. If it's more comfortable, close your eyes to receive. Then write whatever comes to you—with no judgment or editing. If you are visual and images come, write what you see. If you hear an internal voice, small or large, write what you hear. If you have thoughts, body sensations, or emotional knowing, take notes. You are chronicling your expansion, a wondrous winding road, a treasure that is all yours.

7

The Parable of Intergalactic Force

The Fable

Note: This chapter is in parable form to express the idea that once one opens to receive intuitive material from self and others, one must take precaution to only allow in that which is of the highest qualities of what I call the supreme genius of love and light. There are wafts of negativity not of your making that do come at you from others' fields of vibration and/or other consciousness not of a density to be seen.

WHAT HAPPENED long ago still affects us today. Eons ago there was a visitation from an Intergalactic Force, a consciousness that electrically rewired thoughts and awareness.

This consciousness infiltrated our systems against our will. It also fermented in some plant and animal consciousness. In short, it upset the world order.

We grew filled with unrest, disease, and despair. As there are forces of unrest, disease, and despair still here, we need Earthlings to request them to depart.

Those who decided to birth themselves here with the volition to cause havoc still reside. After they have made your acquaintance, they can depart. They want us to know just who they are. Their goal was to have fun, much the way a hacker might take over your computer. They saw excitement in the unrest, disease, and despair.

They came to show us their ways. They do not know about love. They have no such emotion where they are from. They use "brainpower" as a toy for enjoyment. They cannot fathom our experience of loving regard. They have lived inside our thoughts for a very long time.

They were hoping this day would never occur. Please allow them to introduce themselves. They read minds. They read energy. Now that we have found them out, the intergalactic police has ushered all of them to go. Yet, as stated, some of them were grown here, into plant, animal, and mineral.

They have purpose here. They cannot leave unless every one of us, all of our consciousness, prays for them to do so.

Even they wonder what love would be like. They know we crave it, long for it, and wish upon stars for such a thing as love. They know that there are songs, art, and literature with substructures and plots all designed in love. They cannot understand why. They can only enjoy the ride of suffice or sufficient. They know nothing that resembles love.

They ask that we not follow their ways; only those coming from their galaxy can begin to imagine their consciousness. They do not have strongholds in any other galaxy but ours and our Earth. We are similar in construction. We are similar in our standards, but their emotional structure does not resemble ours. They know only suffice and sufficient.

They would prefer we not ask them to leave and instead realize the benefit of the dark void of love. They want to share their names; they are the Volitariat of the Oplisustwon. That will mean nothing to us, as we do not have the same vocabulary.

They are experienced in a culture of decay, destruction, and rebirth; however, they do not regard emotion. They are metallic, industrial, and ever changing.

We, out of love, care about time and consistency. We pray to live lifetimes together.

Our love inspires us to live longer, fuller, deeper commitments to time.

EXERCISE 7: OPEN YOUR HEART

Induction to Meditation

Please see page xvii.

Personalize Your Practice

BEGINNER – This parable is about negativity. If we all worked to neutralize it, we would shift world consciousness. Our Earth world has become contaminated on so many levels, from the way we think to the way we have become distanced from nature.

We take on these exercises to help us, our inner world, and the way we connect. As we vibrate at higher and higher frequencies, we allow for the expansion of our world at large. Just taking care of your self helps the whole.

MASTER – What you resist might just come at you harder. In this critical-mass moment of negativity, it is difficult to feel assured that if we indeed took down the walls of defense and protection, we would still be protected. How will one believe if there aren't quantifiable results? Yet there aren't quantifiable results until you decide to take down the walls and live in trust.

Even if you cannot believe it, just dare. Say: "I invite that which is of the highest qualities of love and light to guide my positive evolution."

PARTNER – If one subscribes to consciousness being eternal, it alters that person's view on survival and competition. If competition arises in the group, it might be the egos, not readied yet to become supported. While our bodies, our nature, and our beliefs are to be valued, you are now going through a huge shift to allow for your world view to be shaken. Keep your heart open to yourself and others, so that the energy of the universe can flow through you.

DATE _____

PLACE _____

TIME _____

WHAT IS MINE TO DO?

Ask the expansive part of yourself.

_____

_____

_____

_____

_____

_____

_____

_____

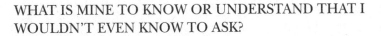

WHAT IS MINE TO KNOW OR UNDERSTAND THAT I WOULDN'T EVEN KNOW TO ASK?

You are asking your Highest Self to be open to that which you may never have imagined. You are asking to see beyond your customary beliefs, ideas, and construction. Leave room for the possibility of receiving answers in both conventional and unconventional ways.

HOW CAN I LOVE MYSELF BEST RIGHT NOW?

As if you are listening to a friend, stay empty, feel, see, hear, know. If it's more comfortable, close your eyes to receive. Then write whatever comes to you—with no judgment or editing. If you are visual and images come, write what you see. If you hear an internal voice, small or large, write what you hear. If you have thoughts, body sensations, or emotional knowing, take notes. You are chronicling your expansion, a wondrous winding road, a treasure that is all yours.

What might I do to fully open my heart?

Am I ready to take down walls of protection that no longer serve my new ability for undefended love?

May I request rewiring for openhearted love of self and other at the same time?

Begin your automatic writing. Review.

Remember: if at any time negative or resistant feelings or thoughts wash over you, write and ask for more understanding. Keep pursuing understanding, knowing that you are expanding from customary and previous expression. Comfort yourself and repeat the top of the exercise. Begin again. Be gentle and loving. All information is valid.

8

Sit Back and Love

SIT BACK and Love to see the benefit of a new, natural peace that is

Effortless
Radiant
Calm
Joyful
Exquisite

After negativity is looked at squarely, it is time to integrate yourself into love.

We now just sit back and love.

EXERCISE 8: MAKING LEMONADE OUT OF LEMONS

Try now to imagine yourself calmed by or in water: morning dew, mist, rain, a bath, a brook, a river, a waterfall, a hot tub, a pool, a lake, and so forth. Whatever will add to your tranquility best. Then ask:

Dear Highest Self,

What is mine to do to become unburdened?

How did the following aspects of my expression help me grow: chaos, resistance, disease, despair, defamation?

How might I look at this growth as exquisite?

How have I made lemonade from my lemons?

What difficulties have shaped or informed the best parts of me?

Have I exhausted my need to grow from fear?

Am I ready to live in a peace that is calm, joyful, radiant, effortless, and exquisite?

Begin your automatic writing. Review.

Remember: if at any time negative or resistant feelings or thoughts wash over you, write and ask for more understanding. Keep pursuing insight, knowing that you are rescuing yourself from customary and previous ways of problem solving.

Have no distress looking into the shadow sides of your material, for you are allowing in the sacredness of both the light and the dark.

While continuing the pursuit of your answers through visualizing, meditating, and expanding, call on that which is of love and light, that which is here for your Highest Good. Keep re-sourcing that part of you that loves yourself.

Comfort yourself. Re-enter or sense the imaginary water and repeat the preparation to meditation induction exercise at the top of the chapter. Begin again. Be gentle and loving. If answers slip away, close your eyes, slow your breathing, feel yourself in the water, and inquire again.

Water is an electrical conductor. Alternate realms are often electromagnetic fields. The water of our body, as well as the water element, assist the conductivity of reception.

All people receive intuitive information differently. You are the primary interpreter of what is yours to decipher.

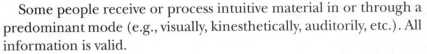

Some people receive or process intuitive material in or through a predominant mode (e.g., visually, kinesthetically, auditorily, etc.). All information is valid.

All people have a speed and tempo that works best for them, whether it's the speed of awareness, or the swiftness with which you care to work the exercises.

With invitation to your new expanding self comes the responsibility to employ self-inquiry (i.e., "What does my body need to eat?" "Do I need more sleep?" etc.).

This new time is for being intuitively vigilant about everything in your life, across the board: body health, feelings, thoughts, work, personal relationships, home, spiritual practice, and so forth. Invite yourself to automatic writing on your own time frame.

Making a choice to relinquish fear in one's day-to-day living radically shifts the whole perspective of one's world. It is often not fathomable.

Those of us who came from the belief, "If I don't have fear, then I don't have life," can actually attain a richer life when motivated by that which is our mission, purpose, or joy. The fuel of life becomes the passion, the co-creation for you to fulfill.

Even if some obstruction rears, try to see it as put there for you to grow, not as being done *to* you. The issue is for a reason, a season, or a lifetime, but there is "lemonade" to be made.

Induction to Meditation

Please see page xvii.

Personalize Your Practice

BEGINNER – Automatic writing is a great way to detoxify, purify, witness, neutralize, and cleanse. Sitting with each question from a Higher Ground (not just from your head) enlists unconscious material to flow forward to consciousness.

Honoring each question could take a very long time, so keep your notes in order. Revisit on an as-needed basis. These are all points on an upward graph toward self-love, feeling your power, and forgiveness.

In order to have peace, calm, joy, radiance, and effortless and exquisite belief about your self, we re-source, again connect, to that which is in love with our self, so as to shed all the anger and resentment. Which doesn't mean it evaporates, but we are not perseverating in it, we are not dwelling in it, we are not chewing on it like cud. We don't allow it to take up real estate in our heads, rethinking and looping in persistent negativity. We let go of the old that does not foster us forward and we enter the positive system.

MASTER – Often our family of origin informs a great deal of our growth, as it was the original imprint. If one supposes that at a soul level we picked our family of origin, or adopted family, as intimates to best grow with, from a soul level, you might inquire, "Why?"

Ponder what was happening in utero, even before imprinting.

We needed mother or birth mother for our survival. We connected to her vibratory state in oneness. If mother/birth mother was, let's say, anxious, when we try to now re-source and regulate our self out of a difficult internal state, we might vibrate anxiety, because that is "mother," the anthem of sustenance.

Create a ceremony to give the difficult states back to our parents.

If they are deceased, they are only allowed to guide you on your terms, not from their old paradigm. Only the highest vibrations of consciousness come in to match you, to support you, to push you further. High consciousness is not dense; they/it can evolve very quickly, yet they require our rich experience of the physical world to make the changes permanent. This earth school and our bodies are not to be squandered. There is a symbiotic exchange from each realm to the next. We grow together, evolving anew.

PARTNER – Eye contact while with an open heart can be very reparative. If the group is not romantically bound, know that spiritual feelings can often be mistaken for sexual feelings. Try not to act on your new feelings without meticulous self-inventory.

If after each question each member is silent to retrieve the answer, have an agreed-upon method by which you wait for each member to complete. Try not breaking up the group, as it is an energy field of exchange and love, until each member has completed the agreed-upon assignment.

There may be a decision to let the group be open-ended for all to get as much time as needed, or for each to get equal regulated time. As these sharings are deeply personal, abide by group ethics, honor each person's time, and be sure everyone is emotionally safe.

DATE _____

PLACE _____

TIME _____

WHAT IS MINE TO DO?

Ask the expansive part of yourself.

_____

_____

_____

_____

_____

_____

WHAT IS MINE TO KNOW OR UNDERSTAND THAT I WOULDN'T EVEN KNOW TO ASK?

You are asking your Highest Self to be open to that which you may never have imagined. You are asking to see beyond your customary beliefs, ideas, and construction. Leave room for the possibility of receiving answers in both conventional and unconventional ways.

_____

_____

_____

_____

_____

HOW CAN I LOVE MYSELF BEST RIGHT NOW?

As if you are listening to a friend, stay empty, feel, see, hear, know. If it's more comfortable, close your eyes to receive. Then write whatever comes to you—with no judgment or editing. If you are visual and images come, write what you see. If you hear an internal voice, small or large, write what you hear. If you have thoughts, body sensations, or emotional knowing, take notes. You are chronicling your expansion, a wondrous winding road, a treasure that is all yours.

_____

_____

_____

_____

9

Leave the Impermanence of Time

"LEAVE" MEANS TO HAVE FUN. Let us explain. This book is a channeled book from guidance, perhaps that should be stated. Just as you are now an open receiver to the most expansive vast parts of you and the plurality that guides you, so was this book. We come with an understanding of the impermanence of time. If that is understood, then there is nothing but "leaving" and "leaving."

We range our growth through realms, and we alternate our existence through growth.

First we are on the dream plane, then we are on the etheric plane, then we are on the dense plane, then we are on the interdimensional realms of parallel time growth. We know because there is bleed-through.

You can be here now and a flash of another time echoes through your head. You seem to have memory collide with "now." This is consciousness that is being played out by something that was set in motion while you were still there. Either you had a potential that is still riding the consciousness there, or you connected to consciousness there and are still playing a part in it and its growth there.

"LEAVE" is the mutable existence we have.

We are in this dense realm primarily when we come through to be born, but there is so much more. We are all places at all times and can join others as well.

There is the déjà vu flash of perception that contains a glimpse of the past that is now being played out in the dense, or a glimpse of the dream-plane past that is now being played out in the dense, or a glimpse of a premonition that is being played out in the dense of now.

Cross realms can contain bleed-through from coexistence or parallel existence, where we have gossamer visions or perceptions or memories that play out in our daily, predominantly linear Earth memory.

"Reasonable awareness" is an allowance for such occurrences to be yours and no one else's because of the infinite ways you are unique. Your reasonable awareness is different from another's with perception, unique expression, and experiences. Listen, watch, see—this is the art of mastering, experiencing, and expressing.

God is the Infinite appreciator of mastering, experiencing, and expressing of love of self and other at the same time. ("Other" is all consciousness.) Love is the opening door.

EXERCISE 9: LOVE IS THE KEY WE MUST TURN

What are the ways my thoughts and visions waft through my perceptions?

At some un-understandable moment, have I suddenly remembered a place I visited long ago?

Have I experienced a memory of old dream material or a flash glimpse of future potential?

Have I lived out those premonitions?

What is my belief around parallel universes?

If I am more vast than my corporeal body, how might I best understand it for myself?

What is my way to appreciate my own mastering, experiencing, and expressing?
What is my difference or unique expression and experience?
How do I cross realms?

Induction to Meditation

Please see page xvii

Personalize Your Practice

BEGINNER – It is liberating to feel like you are not just tied to a daily, bodily experience. If we pay attention, we can start perceiving in new ways. For example: You will be thinking of someone not in your regular circle of friends, maybe someone you hadn't thought about for years, and all of a sudden you will get an email from them. Pay attention to who was the sender and who was the receiver. Who acted first? Yes, those intuitive synchronicities happen in your regular circle of friends; it's just easier to see when a distant contact makes it so apparent how connected we all are, and how intuitive. Our culture is constructed to not pay attention. You will begin to see without your eyes and hear without your ears. You will begin to feel wafts of energy, and smell what also may not be around.

The difference between a hallucination and a spiritual experience is that a hallucination is fleeting, whereas a spiritual experience is long-lasting in memory and detail. We absolutely know where we were when we lived it, and can recall the events with enduring accuracy.

MASTER – Harness all the anonymous, not-so-anonymous, and generous consciousness that works on your behalf, for your greatest good, by requesting in a prayerful state that the Divine work with you in ways you feel are best for you. Be a co-creator with the Divine energies that want, desire, and evolve through assistance to you.

(Continued)

Inquire, when events take place, as to why they do.

Try to stay unattached to the outcome. The less attached you are, the more clear the information will be.

Once the light and love are of you, all is on track for your growth toward understanding the ways of the worlds.

PARTNER – If your partner is going through a snag, ask if you have permission to send love and light, angels, healing, or whatever is comfortable for them to receive within their beliefs. See if after they receive the transmission they report feeling the energy. Perhaps this is an example of alternate assistance not from the dense realm.

If they have difficulty receiving, it might be worth looking at the idea of "receiving" for this individual. If control or uncertainty are important for fueling their daily living, they may need your loving assistance to help them see their setup.

Trust that just showing up on your own behalf toward your own expansion is honoring your timing. Nothing more is needed or required. Everyone has their own timing. Everyone is perfect.

DATE

PLACE

TIME

WHAT IS MINE TO DO?

Ask the expansive part of yourself.

WHAT IS MINE TO KNOW OR UNDERSTAND THAT I WOULDN'T EVEN KNOW TO ASK?

You are asking your Highest Self to be open to that which you may never have imagined. You are asking to see beyond your customary beliefs, ideas, and construction. Leave room for the possibility of receiving answers in both conventional and unconventional ways.

HOW CAN I LOVE MYSELF BEST RIGHT NOW?

As if you are listening to a friend, stay empty, feel, see, hear, know. If it's more comfortable, close your eyes to receive. Then write whatever comes to you—with no judgment or editing. If you are visual and images come, write what you see. If you hear an internal voice, small or large, write what you hear. If you have thoughts, body sensations, or emotional knowing, take notes. You are chronicling your expansion, a wondrous winding road, a treasure that is all yours.

10

Be Of Source

BE OF SOURCE. All will unfold. Never worry. Love is all around you. Feel it. Others may not feel it for centuries. Some will feel it right away.

EXERCISE 10: BE VAST

My body is the vehicle of this lifetime. I will cherish and honor my body for all that it has done for me.

Please may my body come forward and let me know just what it needs to sustain best health?

Best exercise each day?

Best foods each day?

How best may my body be a conduit for intuitive material?

Does my body even want to participate in such events?

What are the ways my body does want to participate?

How might I finely attune to these new energies?

(Please keep a running dialogue, as your body might go through changes and revisions on what "best" is from one day to the next, one month to the next, even one moment to the next. Stay open and flexible, as often we are taken on a circuitous route to new results.)

Induction to Meditation

Please see page xvii.

Personalize Your Practice

BEGINNER – Since the body is the vehicle for dense perception in linear time, as well as the primary tool to read out intuitive information, we are re-upping the body's commitment to go universal. You are attending to your body's needs to make it a more ready vessel for your expansion by learning what it requires to more finely attune to energies operating on its behalf.

Please keep honoring and thanking your body for all it has given you. If you get a cold or the flu, know that when in transformation, we sometimes need a cleanse. Tired, compromised, or diseased cells will slough off. Look at the gift of the cleanse and know that your body is improving.

MASTER – You may have received intuitive information that your body needs, requires, or enjoys water, nature, healings (such as acupuncture, craniosacral, etc.). When your body is receiving light/healing, please remember to prayerfully inquire to the high consciousness of your surroundings, or to the ancients that brought through these healings, whether there is even more intuitive information. When in a relaxed and receiving state, we are bolstered by the energies supplying the healing. Often they will come forward with intuitive signs and messages.

PARTNER – There is group intuition, where a few or all are receiving messages at the same time. As the group knits itself closer and closer, you may find yourself sharing complementary intuitive material. Discover together how you each work with that which comes forth. It will illuminate how you may work as a group or alone.

DATE _____

PLACE _____

TIME _____

WHAT IS MINE TO DO?

Ask the expansive part of yourself.

_____

_____

_____

_____

WHAT IS MINE TO KNOW OR UNDERSTAND THAT I WOULDN'T EVEN KNOW TO ASK?

You are asking your Highest Self to be open to that which you may never have imagined. You are asking to see beyond your customary beliefs, ideas, and construction. Leave room for the possibility of receiving answers in both conventional and unconventional ways.

_____

_____

_____

_____

_____

_____

HOW CAN I LOVE MYSELF BEST RIGHT NOW?

As if you are listening to a friend, stay empty, feel, see, hear, know. If it's more comfortable, close your eyes to receive. Then write whatever comes to you—with no judgment or editing. If you are visual and images come, write what you see. If you hear an internal voice, small or large, write what you hear. If you have thoughts, body sensations, or emotional knowing, take notes. You are chronicling your expansion, a wondrous winding road, a treasure that is all yours.

11

Cellular Rejuvenation

SUPPORT HAS COME. We are now enhanced for our own self-expansion beyond what we initially thought possible. We are partners to a beginning of cellular rejuvenation and enjoyment that will be regarded as phenomenal.

Because we are physical beings of this Earth, the interaction must transpire through all expression. We partner in our vastness to invite in all supports of our highest good: mentally, emotionally, physically, and spiritually.

We call on this support in conventional ways, like prayer or meditation.

Any extra-dimensional or extra-frequency assistance is to be of love and have no agenda but to be of service. They are excited to serve because it makes them feel useful. Just as we visit other places to lovingly offer education or care, they are here to be of assistance.

By living in alternate expressions, they communicate with us through telepathy and silent communication.

We will understand their openhearted gratitude as we can understand how good it makes us feel when we help those in need.

"They" are the consciousness from all realms and worlds. Just as we drop our physical form and our consciousness remains eternal and of purpose, so does that of the animal and plant kingdoms. When calling in service, be broad-minded to all that is there for you.

EXERCISE 11: PHENOMENAL

May I please request loving assistance from all that is of service to my Highest Good to rejuvenate the cells of my body and my thoughts, emotions, or difficult internal states, so that I may forego the unnecessary pain of growth with fear, trials, and tribulations?

May I please have a sneak peek of my future way of being, so that I may not feel resistant to my new expansion?

How might that work?

Induction to Meditation

Please see page xvii.

Personalize Your Practice

BEGINNER – We ask our Highest Self for a sneak preview of our future, so that we are less resistant to our own expansion. We are reassuring our ego, as the watchdog of our original patterning, to be assured that we will never unknow what we already know. We are honoring and grateful for all that we are, and now in expanding across all expression, it is a carrot to imagine a potential of you that you have no reference for.

MASTER – You might feel like indulging in a day of rest, where you are being revamped, rewired, and restructured energetically. Luxuriate in the rest. You might be called to follow cravings, to enjoy your body's knowings. Remember to check in with your Highest Self so as to solidify that these knowings are coming from your highest source of divine intuition.

(Continued)

When in group settings where there is a great deal of outside psychic debris, take a volitional time-out to not only recalibrate, but also to send only the highest consciousness of love and light into the room. Build a field of love and light for you and others.

PARTNERS – There is a parable where everyone in a group is blindfolded and asked to touch and describe what is in front of them. What they cannot see is an elephant. Each describes their part: one the tail, one the ear, one the trunk. It all seems as though they are touching very different objects, yet they are just feeling different parts of the same elephant.

In sharing group material, leave the potential for each person to be describing his or her part of the same whole. Find a reflection of yourself in each person's sharing. Build compassion for yourself through others, and build compassion for others through you.

DATE

PLACE

TIME

WHAT IS MINE TO DO?

Ask the expansive part of yourself.

WHAT IS MINE TO KNOW OR UNDERSTAND THAT I WOULDN'T EVEN KNOW TO ASK?

You are asking your Highest Self to be open to that which you may never have imagined. You are asking to see beyond your customary beliefs, ideas, and construction. Leave room for the possibility of receiving answers in both conventional and unconventional ways.

HOW CAN I LOVE MYSELF BEST RIGHT NOW?

As if you are listening to a friend, stay empty, feel, see, hear, know. If it's more comfortable, close your eyes to receive. Then write whatever comes to you—with no judgment or editing. If you are visual and images come, write what you see. If you hear an internal voice, small or large, write what you hear. If you have thoughts, body sensations, or emotional knowing, take notes. You are chronicling your expansion, a wondrous winding road, a treasure that is all yours.

12

Speaking Words of Wisdom

AS YOU CONTINUE your transformation, many loved ones and friends around you will be going through many of their own issues.

In some cases you may have customarily given counsel to their process and let them lean on you in a good way. In other cases you may have pulled back to let them flower, to become better, stronger individuals.

Right now is a very important time for you. Inquire every day, "What is mine to do?" The gift you are giving yourself is a more deeply connected, intuitive you. Time alone or resting may be advised. Keep honoring yourself in this very deep process.

Journal, keeping your notes in order to review them years from now. See the worlds unfold. Take comfort.

EXERCISE 12: REALIGNING

When asking, "What is mine to do today?" reflect on each situation that is pulling on your energy.

Ask, "What is mine to do today?" (You are asking with respect to each individual and/or situation, as you and your relationship to yourself and your body, family, friends, and work are all realigning.)

Inquire, "What might I need to know that I may not even know to ask?"

(Asking this question serves to open you beyond previous patterns and constructs, while inviting alternate realms to give you information as well.)

Make a committed inventory. (Ask and write for each heading.)

Body: _____

_____

Family: _____

_____

Friends/Personal Relationships: _____

_____

Work: _____

_____

Induction to Meditation

Please see page xvii.

Personalize Your Practice

BEGINNER – You are continuing your rigorous self-examination from the now-formed plurality of you, so as not to nurture or expend energy to your own detriment, or, conversely, to find the courage to bravely enter situations you may never have dared go into before.

Each reexamination from your Highest Self further allows for change, moment to moment, as to who the new you is and what the new you needs.

This is much like looking at the same painting over and over and seeing something new each time, or taking Social Studies and History in 4th, 5th, and 6th grades. Each time you understand at deeper and deeper levels.

MASTER – Charging in pervasively and committedly to your vastness can sometimes feel like a free-fall. You are being asked to trust yourself while you assimilate contradictions, balance logic and creativity, unify people with divergent agendas, and more.

Intuitive information can come in erratically, profusely, poetically, cryptically, or straightforwardly, and can range from the ridiculous to the sublime. The Divine seemingly has a sense of humor, and sometimes the jokes may appear at your expense. Trust.

There can be lags in connection, but it may be that you are in need of integrating all that has gone on before moving forward again. Trust in the perfection of ALL. Know that your continued commitment to your own personal transformation will yield a return. Part of the joy of living is the unfolding.

PARTNER – Whether alone or in a group, reaching higher meditation states could actually change your brain patterns and help you better problem-solve.

In partnership, if there are problems that arise, try to stay in your meditative state, while "going in" on your self, then others. Use your bi-location knowledge, even if they are in front of you. Ask your Highest Self quite a few times, so as to try to not operate from projection (a defense mechanism whereby we suppose or assume what the other is going through). You can sense after a while when you are operating from your Highest Self. Go back and forth in systematic inquiry, with meticulous introspection from your Highest Self. When there is charge and hurt feelings, it may take time and distance before elevated prayerful inquiry is answered. Know that the process is sometimes the gift. Finally coming together with improved communication and self-awareness supported by the grace of the Divine is also a blessed treasure.

DATE

PLACE

TIME

WHAT IS MINE TO DO?

Ask the expansive part of yourself.

WHAT IS MINE TO KNOW OR UNDERSTAND THAT I WOULDN'T EVEN KNOW TO ASK?

You are asking your Highest Self to be open to that which you may never have imagined. You are asking to see beyond your customary beliefs, ideas,

and construction. Leave room for the possibility of receiving answers in both conventional and unconventional ways.

HOW CAN I LOVE MYSELF BEST RIGHT NOW?

As if you are listening to a friend, stay empty, feel, see, hear, know. If it's more comfortable, close your eyes to receive. Then write whatever comes to you—with no judgment or editing. If you are visual and images come, write what you see. If you hear an internal voice, small or large, write what you hear. If you have thoughts, body sensations, or emotional knowing, take notes. You are chronicling your expansion, a wondrous winding road, a treasure that is all yours.

13

Going Universal

*T*HERE ARE AWAKENINGS or urges that may come over you. Reflect on these. Ask all that is holy to you if they are moments to be used to journal, write, and/or meditate. You are now in a multidimensional universal mode of sending and receiving. These are precious and rich times.

EXERCISE 13: NEVER SQUANDER THE MOMENTS

Dear Highest Self,
What is this moment best used for?
   What, who, why am I feeling like this?
   What might I need to know that I would not even know to ask at a universal level of sending and receiving?

Induction to Meditation

Please see page xvii.

Personalize Your Practice

BEGINNER – There are unwanted aspects of self or devastating, horrible occurrences in the world that might seem to be better made sense of when we use alternate realms to help. The feeling of oneness is difficult to master as a constant, but keep trying.

Stay centered no matter what is thrown at you. Find your heart and ask "Why?" from your highest, most sacred place. In going "up" and "in" to self-inquire for an elevated prayer state, over and over, we flex the muscle that leads us to more accessibility.

These are rich times, where all is explored for meaning.

When we are in a multidimensional mode of receiving, we begin to integrate, awaken, and understand potentials that never occurred to us before.

It is an aspiration to feel oneness all the time, but precious is the joy from trying.

MASTER – When in daily living, try to operate on all realms at the same time, living as though in prayer every moment. Each event is infused with elevating your usual and customary role in simultaneously wondering if this is still the way the new expanded you is at your best.

When with others, try to have your Highest Self in interaction with their Highest Self. Use internal imagining of spreading the light and love to all events, before, during, and after they take place. You are a pump for the light. Receive the light and love as well. In quiet stillness, feel that which you give circle back to you. These are very subtle exchanges, but they are magnificent, magnanimous, and monumental in reach.

PARTNER – Each person's connection to their Highest Self is so personal. Each person's belief about their own multidimensional vastness is deeply unique. The paradox is that no one is the glory of you, yet we are all one. Use the partner experience to ponder that together.

DATE _____

PLACE _____

TIME _____

WHAT IS MINE TO DO?
Ask the expansive part of yourself.

_____

_____

_____

_____

_____

WHAT IS MINE TO KNOW OR UNDERSTAND THAT I WOULDN'T EVEN KNOW TO ASK?

You are asking your Highest Self to be open to that which you may never have imagined. You are asking to see beyond your customary beliefs, ideas, and construction. Leave room for the possibility of receiving answers in conventional and unconventional ways.

_____

_____

_____

_____

_____

HOW CAN I LOVE MYSELF BEST RIGHT NOW?

As if you are listening to a friend, stay empty, feel, see, hear, know. If it's more comfortable, close your eyes to receive. Then write whatever comes to you—with no judgment or editing. If you are visual and images come, write what you see. If you hear an internal voice, small or large, write what you hear. If you have thoughts, body sensations, or emotional knowing, take notes. You are chronicling your expansion, a wondrous winding road, a treasure that is all yours.

14

Backlash

*T*HE NEGATIVE SYSTEM thrives on resistance, defiance, fear, division, aloneness, chaos, confusion, and rejection.

If we are to join with ourselves and others in the Positive System, then we might start by wondering what it might be like to live:

- With an open heart
- Being of service to each other
- In connection to others through collaboration, improvisation, inspiration, humor, and co-creation, only experiencing pain for growth's sake.

Exchanging expression through laughter, loving regard, joy, health, peace, elevated DNA, breakthroughs in consciousness, and romantic love coming from the negative into the positive requires an honoring of all modes of expression. Take that moment to honor all that you were and all that you are. There might be a backlash from the ego, as watchdog of the old patterns, to fight, freeze, or try to instigate "flight" through obfuscation, interruption, or making us think we must do. ("Doing" is action that takes us away from our Highest knowing.)

Sometimes these critical-mass moments—when we feel untethered to our guidance or unsure as to whether to proceed or even how to act—may be the biggest gifts of awareness.

EXERCISE 14: DEMANDMENTS

Is there anything I might need to integrate immediately to be on course?

My demands are the following:

(Make a list of all that you want to attain: health, love, friendship, work, and the spiritual. In this exercise you are demanding to co-create your life with all that is of service to your Highest Self again, so as to see if more expanded understandings have occurred since you last inquired.)

_____

_____

_____

_____

Induction to Meditation

Please see page xvii

Personalize Your Practice

BEGINNER – "Elevated DNA" means that you have requested through prayer that your entire body be healed. For example, let's say that in your "demands" you meditated and received that your health is to stay strong, balanced, and disease-free. You are elevating your DNA just by meditating, inquiring, and praying for your being.

"Demand" or "Demandment" is not selfish, but in regard for self. In loving our self, all else follows.

We are no longer in plea, wish, desire, wanting, or craving; we are demanding, erect, and ready and in trust to our co-creation with our Highest Self.

It is us taking our power. When writing out your "demandments," use direct, positive words, not double negatives. Be clear, forthright, and powerful.

MASTER – It is common that when we begin to transform at the causal roots of our pattern, the negative does intensify. Often there is backlash; we might feel pushed up against the walls of our patterns, so hating where we are, even though it is exquisitely all in beautiful order, so that we risk the fear of the change.

There is an adage of a man who keeps stepping into an open manhole, until the day he learns to walk around it. Your awareness makes you say, "I am not going to do that again."

PARTNER – Listening to others with acceptance rather than reaction is required, so that you both really value, see, honor, and understand each other at the same time. It doesn't mean there will be perfect attunement, but that there is a pledge or demandment to live like that. As you go "up" and "in," you bypass the mundane and begin working from a vibratory flow of oneness. Every exchange is a prayer or invocation. The potential for attunement is greatly

(Continued)

increased. There is an agreement, spoken or unspoken, to attain a High Ground connection, whereby even if someone says something offensive, there is a better chance to see where they might be coming from, to shift the energy and elevate the exchange.

When in prayerful states, your high brain is enlisted, your fear center is disengaged, and you know more clearly who you are…that you are not going to get swallowed up, or disavowed, or, when energy comes over you that causes you to get defensive, feel misunderstood, disrespected, or rejected. In prayerful states, we trust ourselves and others at the same time.

The distinction is not prayer vs. meditation, but that both are at the highest vibratory invocation of the highest quality of love and light before exchanges of sending and receiving.

DATE _____

PLACE _____

TIME _____

WHAT IS MINE TO DO?

Ask the expansive part of yourself.

_____

_____

_____

_____

_____

_____

WHAT IS MINE TO KNOW OR UNDERSTAND THAT I WOULDN'T EVEN KNOW TO ASK?

You are asking your Highest Self to be open to that which you may never have imagined. You are asking to see beyond your customary beliefs, ideas, and construction. Leave room for the possibility of receiving answers in both conventional and unconventional ways.

_____

_____

_____

_____

HOW CAN I LOVE MYSELF BEST RIGHT NOW?

As if you are listening to a friend, stay empty, feel, see, hear, know. If it's more comfortable, close your eyes to receive. Then write whatever comes to you—with no judgment or editing. If you are visual and images come, write what you see. If you hear an internal voice, small or large, write what you hear. If you have thoughts, body sensations, or emotional knowing, take notes. You are chronicling your expansion, a wondrous winding road, a treasure that is all yours.

_____

_____

_____

_____

_____

15

All Ways

REVIEWING YOUR NEWLY requested co-created life (see Chapter 3) also includes the honoring of ancestral patterns passed down through unspoken messages, repetition compulsions, behaviors, attachment strategies, methods of communication, conflict resolution styles, and DNA.

Expanding beyond exhausted agreements, or that which is customary and usual, brings an honoring of all that you have learned from that which you inherited, whether directly or indirectly.

"Honor" is to be in gratitude. Gratitude is acknowledging what was indeed given, and giving thanks for all the growth and learning that inspired who you are today, despite whether or not you would have consciously chosen what was given if asked now.

EXERCISE 15: ANCESTRAL TIES UNBOUND

The following is a guided imagery exercise. Stay very open to all of your expression as valid. Ask that nothing stand in the way of your expansion. For the sake of this meditation, all of the material is metaphorically "you." If for any reason any of the imagery or air balloons are not "you," design your own imagery toward the same result.

You are standing in the basket of a beautiful air balloon tethered to the ground by large stakes and rope. Millions of beautiful filaments hold the basket to the glorious colored air balloon above your head.

The millions of filaments represent your internal thought processes, emotional states, and body health. The filaments represent the current people in your life: loved ones, family, friends, work acquaintances, and strangers who impact you. The filaments represent the ancestral lines and spiritual connections that may guide, protect, and direct you.

Take make-believe beautiful scissors and cut all the filaments, so as to sever the old patterns, connections, and constructs. Now take a long inhale and, with your imagination, invite all that you cut to come back in, but on your new terms, the terms you designed and co-created in Exercise 13.

Now the millions of new filaments represent the new internal thought processes, emotional states, and body health you want to start living. The new filaments represent the people in your life: loved ones, family, friends, work acquaintances, and strangers who will begin to impact you in new ways. The new filaments now represent the ancestral lines and spiritual connections that will come upon your invitation to guide, protect, and direct your best interests.

Watch as all the filaments come back anew, in brilliant and radiant colors. Remove the stakes and let your balloon soar to great heights. Enjoy the symbolic new ride of your life.

Induction to Meditation

Please see page xvii.

Personalize Your Practice

BEGINNER – "Repetition Compulsion" is a Freudian concept around volitional attraction to that which is not good for us. Freud postulates that we are repeating the attraction not to satisfy masochistic tendencies, but because we are unconsciously seeking victory over some piece of unresolved dynamic that resides inside of our psychological construction.

MASTER – If one needs control or security, one might be blocking one's own expansion. In needing to know what the future holds, we block the unknown.

In wanting terra firma over the existential angst of the unknown, we impair our capacity to be a receiver.

The unknown is greater than you can imagine from the old setup of you.

As a personality construct, some of us specialize in being givers, whether information, material, or emotional support. Sometimes the giving is a defense against the unknown. As the giver, we are in control, superior, knowing what will likely happen next. Also we are often addicted to doing and uncomfortable with change.

Some of us specialize in receiving, often too scared to act and more assured through waiting.

Balance where we are through gratitude, equally giving and receiving simultaneously. Accept universal information, which is often not tangible or seen. When living in the vastness of our own expansion, so open, so empty, we live in trust. The balance of giving and receiving is our capacity to love and be loved.

PARTNER – "Attachment Strategies," developed by Mary Ainsworth, are constellations of connection behavior formed with and through one's relationships with one's primary caregivers. Some of us form secure attachments and are usually more capable of loving relationships; many others have had trauma or fissures, informing different qualities to their capacity to attach.

DATE _____

PLACE _____

TIME _____

WHAT IS MINE TO DO?

Ask the expansive part of yourself.

_____

_____

_____

_____

WHAT IS MINE TO KNOW OR UNDERSTAND THAT I WOULDN'T EVEN KNOW TO ASK?

You are asking your Highest Self to be open to that which you may never have imagined. You are asking to see beyond your customary beliefs, ideas, and construction. Leave room for the possibility of receiving answers in both conventional and unconventional ways.

_____

_____

_____

_____

_____

_____

HOW CAN I LOVE MYSELF BEST RIGHT NOW?

As if you are listening to a friend, stay empty, feel, see, hear, know. If it's more comfortable, close your eyes to receive. Then write whatever comes to you—with no judgment or editing. If you are visual and images come, write what you see. If you hear an internal voice, small or large, write what you hear. If you have thoughts, body sensations, or emotional knowing, take notes. You are chronicling your expansion, a wondrous winding road, a treasure that is all yours.

16

The Explorer

ALL OF CREATION depends on the Positive System to get enforced. There are many who will take this for granted, tossing it away as a passing fad. They do not realize the physics of what we are trying to pull off. None of us are prepared to live a moment longer in a world motivated by dark.

The ramifications are enormous. All individuals must give up their unique quality of growth, as all growth will come from collaboration, inspiration, and improvisation.

All growth will now include two, three, four, or more persons or guidance from an alternate realm. Each theme may not be introduced at the preferred timing; all will be in community.

See the physics greatly alter the state of affairs. See yourself as a positioner to a new world order that reflects a new age of universal love, gratitude, and alliance. People, animals—all of life and consciousness will have new abilities to connect. It will be important to see if that is what others might or will do, as we are all on different thematic courses to attain growth and gains from expression and experience.

Will people share in an agenda of loving regard through mutual experience and expression?

Earthly flesh is necessary to express it all. We are about to start a revolution of physical expression, as all dense reality affects itself and all that is physical.

Are you committed? Just see yourself as having set out in an enormous ship, with a crew, for a new world. Your tenacity is outrageous (i.e., outside of rage). To falter now would mean an empty life.

Your body needs to be prepared and readied for an expression of love and light. You need to find peace in your form. Just that is a big victory. It is time to share the light with each cell.

EXERCISE 16: BODY LOVE

What does my body need now, as fuel, exercise, and acknowledgment to feel loved?

Perhaps start an awareness to reverse unkind or critical thoughts of you.

Perhaps each time you look in the mirror, tell yourself how beautiful and/or how handsome you are, to feel your body's worth.

Take a pause to appreciate your body parts for the lessons they have brought you to date.

Follow your intuitions about eating, sleeping, and exercise. Do not be surprised if your eating, sleeping, and exercise habits change. Know that each moment may bring something new. Keep checking with yourself.

Stay open and fluid for new awareness about your physical self. Stay open to being a physical receiver for different and adventuresome experiences and/or intuitive material. You might be urged to go outside your usual and customary comfort zone.

Induction to Meditation

Please see page xvii.

Personalize Your Practice

BEGINNER/PARTNER – Each theme may not get introduced at the preferred timing; all will be in community. This means that we are not alone in working through many of the themes/issues/values for the betterment of all.

For instance, let's say that part of your work in tackling your journal was "failure." You are tired of feeling like a failure and have been working on that theme. It's been weeks with little progress, then all of a sudden someone comes into your life and says the exact right phrase that opens you up to why you have been afraid of success. Whether it was said to you directly for just you, or was on TV and indirectly affected you greatly, we are all ready to pop open at exactly the moment we are ready to pop.

We are here together all working on similar themes. We evolve together, and as we improve at a quicker pace, those around us shift as well. Hopefully we inspire positive growth, but resistances can emerge. Often the harshest resistance is right before the opening toward expansion, as discussed in Chapter 14.

Issues will not be tackled the hard way anymore. That doesn't mean there will not be pain, but it is not pain with fear or added drama and chaos. We will create more loving environments where we work through that which is needed.

MASTER/PARTNER – See the physics greatly alter the state of affairs. This means one makes a commitment on the spiritual level, but it is lived out on the physical level. The revolution of the Positive System is that our spiritual consciousness has signed on with all other humanity and all other consciousness—animal, plant—to bring in and operate from universal love. The first of us will trudge through the jungle, but as more are in agreement, the physics of momentum will aid in speed.

We all signed up on the etheric, but we consecrate it on the physical. Just having the wish or desire is not enough; we must all live it. The revolution is physical, but it started in the non-physical.

(Continued)

That is why you keep asking your Highest Self, your version of Divine: "Am I committed?" Because the commitment comes first on the spiritual to initiate the trust that it will be brought through the dense physical.

Take another beat to see if there is any part of you—the vast you, the spiritual you, the physical you—that is not committed to a new kind of love in the world, where all consciousness has the ability to connect and grow through loving regard.

DATE _____

PLACE _____

TIME _____

WHAT IS MINE TO DO?

Ask the expansive part of yourself.

_____

_____

_____

_____

WHAT IS MINE TO KNOW OR UNDERSTAND THAT I WOULDN'T EVEN KNOW TO ASK?

You are asking your Highest Self to be open to that which you may never have imagined. You are asking to see beyond your customary beliefs, ideas, and construction. Leave room for the possibility of receiving answers in both conventional and unconventional ways.

_____

_____

_____

_____

_____

_____

HOW CAN I LOVE MYSELF BEST RIGHT NOW?

As if you are listening to a friend, stay empty, and feel, see, hear, know. If it's more comfortable, close your eyes to receive. Then write whatever comes to you—with no judgment or editing. If you are visual and images come, write what you see. If you hear an internal voice, small or large, write what you hear. If you have thoughts, body sensations, or emotional knowing, take notes. You are chronicling your expansion, a wondrous winding road, a treasure that is all yours.

_____

_____

_____

_____

_____

_____

_____

Outside Reflects Inside

*A*LL THAT EXISTS is of light and love because of how one chooses to grow, learn, and love. When value is rendered either personally or in the oneness of being, then all transmutes to love and light. There is usually a mutuality of exchange in each piece of life lived. When looked at deeply, one usually can find it all as quite exquisite and wondrous.

Sometimes our bodies and internal states can take on the transformative lessons we undergo as we shift and expand to the positive system.

Please say prayers for your internal states as well as your body not to take the hit, as there are ways for you to make the shift to the positive system through your growth and experiences on alternate realms, such as the dream plane. In order to imprint the learning and make permanent its effect, journal, write, meditate, and reflect.

Now is the time to calibrate a new internal setting where self-love emanates from an integral feeling of well-being and admiration. How the external world reacts to you is often a reflection of how you are perceived inside yourself. Your outside world reflects your inside world, so to speak.

Now is the time to recalibrate that internal setting. You are nothing but a part of the "isness" and the all. With that in mind, you have recalibrated your being to express and experience predominantly love and light.

All remaining darkness or fears may take some time to remove themselves from your being. In order for you to never unknow what you already know, a so-called "library" is housing your memory outside your body. You do not have to live the dark, but can access your life at any time. All parts of you that no longer actively serve your mental, emotional, physical, and spiritual states, but might be wanted at times to check in or check out, can be put on reserve for you in the ethers. They do not have to live in your person.

All information will be given not through sense memory, but through effortless exchange of loving regard for the past. It will have a being state but will not affect your body, mind, or emotions.

If we request the ability to work with the dark on the interdimensional planes, then the issue becomes keeping the dark active elsewhere. The idea is first to find our own loving regard for self, then care about the dark we have had to live up to this point as a learning toward expansion, then place the experience in a library with access on an as-needed basis.

EXERCISE 17: CREATING THE LIBRARY

List the main memories of times of great remorse, guilt, dread, regret, shame, terror, and so on in a column. To the side of each memory, see if you can find the benefit from each event. Was there a deepening or honing of some of the best parts of you, such as compassion, observational skills, intelligence, or intuition? Did those times ignite a needed course correction? After all is written and regarded in some way for the growth and expansion it most likely afforded, imagine your beautiful library. Open the doors and place all your hardship on the shelf.

Know that you can retrieve those memories and feelings at any time. You are just making a conscious choice not to live with these difficult internal states any longer.

(In the case of missing or mourning loved ones, see Chapter 28.)

Induction to Meditation

Please see page xvii.

Personalize Your Practice

BEGINNER – A "course correction" is when you are motivated to shift direction from where you were headed. Often those who have had near-death experiences (NDEs) will share it as the moment when they knew the new mission or purpose that was now theirs to be had. Working on our journal, we don't have to have a brush with death to make a profound course correction. We are now listening to our vast self, eagerly excited and supple to receive new growth for our Highest Good.

MASTER – Transmuting dark to light using the dream plane requires little more than requesting that your Highest Self, your guidance and your version of the Divine, assist you to make repairs with those situations that are not serving your Highest Good through the dream plane. Trust.

PARTNER – There was much lead-in and foundational exploration leading up to this chapter. Sure, we could flippantly choose to not live out the darkness anymore, but without honoring the past, forgiving the past, and rendering the strength from our past, we don't flower to our fullest.

You, as partners, have an extra gift through the sharing. It is the gift of witness. There is a tremendous power of healing by giving witness. There is no weakness in crying, if that occurs. There is great strength in vulnerability. The tears are holy water blessing the exchange. Make sacred your role, whichever you hold. It is an honor to provide that love.

DATE _____

PLACE _____

TIME _____

WHAT IS MINE TO DO?

Ask the expansive part of yourself.

_____

_____

_____

_____

WHAT IS MINE TO KNOW OR UNDERSTAND THAT I WOULDN'T EVEN KNOW TO ASK?

You are asking your Highest Self to be open to that which you may never have imagined. You are asking to see beyond your customary beliefs, ideas, and construction. Leave room for the possibility of receiving answers in both conventional and unconventional ways.

_____

_____

_____

_____

_____

_____

HOW CAN I LOVE MYSELF BEST RIGHT NOW?

As if you are listening to a friend, stay empty, feel, see, hear, know. If it's more comfortable, close your eyes to receive. Then write whatever comes to you—with no judgment or editing. If you are visual and images come, write what you see. If you hear an internal voice, small or large, write what you hear. If you have thoughts, body sensations, or emotional knowing, take notes. You are chronicling your expansion, a wondrous winding road, a treasure that is all yours.

18

Send in the Battalion

HERE IS THE PLAN for provision. First, never let the dark into your body, mind, emotions, or spirit on all dimensions throughout time, forever, beyond, and always again.

See the dark as a component of shelved material that is of reference. One could read it with the detachment of history. You can relate, but it is not *of* you.

There are justifications to see the world with loving regard for the dark, as it is a force of nature now. Pain is a necessary component of growth, but it is never to contain fear. The amalgamation of pain and fear is at the root of the predominance of the dark.

See yourself as one with the light, and see yourself with information from the dark. There are beings of the multidimensional worlds that have gone into the dark for us, so that they might understand it at its causal roots. They have taken hard hits for us. They have offered themselves as transmuters. Many of them led lives of the dark, and exhausted their commitments of growth from the dark.

Having once been from the dark, they enjoy helping that which wants to transmute from growth from the dark to growth from the light, no matter in which realm or dimension the consciousness resides. The transmuters need assistance from helpers.

They cannot do it by themselves, as most of them are just a past, once-mortal soul consciousness. Transmuters need to be able to address huge energetic forces all at once.

Deployed assistance is sometimes from the very leagues of that which does not want to assist. That which does not want to assist has lived in the light for awhile now and does not want to endure exchanges with the dark. Those now from the light have new commitments to be in, of, and for the light.

Those from the dark, on the other, non-mortal side, that have not yet gone into the light, cannot be trusted to be loyal to the light. They have dropped their body, but not their commitment to learn from the dark.

The animal and plant kingdoms, in their wisdom of many more years on Earth, with far more capacity to transmute harsh conditions to thrive, have all said "YES!" They were great warriors of instinct and very much want to be warriors for the light.

It is their nature to transmute the energies of the subtle. Both on the dense Earth plane and the etheric, animals will come forward.

The cats, the dogs, the birds, the mammals of land and sea will assist in the transmutation. The plants will radiate their light, love, and healing.

Multidimensional beings of all strata and phylum have come together with Mother Earth to begin a new age of love and light.

EXERCISE 18: THE PLAN

When wafts of distress or difficulty come over your thoughts, body, emotions, or spirit, visually conjure your library shelf and place these wafts on the shelf. See yourself as one with the light.

On an as-needed basis, you might require information from the dark. See the dark as a component of shelved material that is of reference. One could read it with the detachment of history. You can relate, but it is not *of* you.

Through guided imagery, call on all the helpers of the light to assist you in bringing the light to any endeavor.

Induction to Meditation

Please see page xvii.

Personalize Your Practice

BEGINNER – If you tend to be the person who feels determination to do it yourself, it is time to receive. If you tend to be down-to-earth, practical, and focused on doing, don't forget to have joy. Accept help with joy, rather than a sense of failure.

In walking into the light, asking for Divine assistance or assistance from that which is bigger than you proves to be reassuring and safe. You will not disappear or un-become. The opposite will occur: you will feel full and completed. Allow for the feelings of well-being to permeate.

MASTER – When in an active state of inquiry, we are bringing in constant assistance. It becomes quicker and quicker to access. You will get to a time when you no longer have to close your eyes, visualize the light, walk into the light. The muscle will be so flexed that a simple, slow inhale of breath will be an abbreviated inroad to your vast self, your Highest Self, and all the Assistance there for you that comes ushering forth.

Every decision will feel more integrated with strength.

There are so many gorgeous ways you could be the bearer of all the new knowledge coming through you with all the Divine help.

PARTNER – It's very hard to have elevated conversation with two defensive people. These exercises bypass everyday defenses. Just say, "Join with me," in request of not just both of your Highest Selves showing up, but, in addition, all the Divine assistance both of you bring. Marvel at the feeling.

DATE _____

PLACE _____

TIME _____

WHAT IS MINE TO DO?

Ask the expansive part of yourself.

_____

_____

_____

_____

WHAT IS MINE TO KNOW OR UNDERSTAND THAT I WOULDN'T EVEN KNOW TO ASK?

You are asking your Highest Self to be open to that which you may never have imagined. You are asking to see beyond your customary beliefs, ideas, and construction. Leave room for the possibility of receiving answers in both conventional and unconventional ways.

_____

_____

_____

_____

_____

_____

HOW CAN I LOVE MYSELF BEST RIGHT NOW?

As if you are listening to a friend, stay empty, feel, see, hear, know. If it's more comfortable, close your eyes to receive. Then write whatever comes to you—with no judgment or editing. If you are visual and images come, write what you see. If you hear an internal voice, small or large, write what you hear. If you have thoughts, body sensations, or emotional knowing, take notes. You are chronicling your expansion, a wondrous winding road, a treasure that is all yours.

Part 2

THE BURNING BUSH

Miraculous Energy, Sacred Light,
Purity, Clarity, Love

19

The Dark Turns In On Itself

*T*HE FABLE CONTINUES. Please understand that constant prayer to invoke the good will be of importance. You are attempting to expunge the dark with their knowing, and they are not happy about leaving. It is true that they must leave when they are found out.

There are forces involved on a grand, ordered scale that will make them leave.

Unless one has called them in, they are not allowed to be around Earth. We were fighting many dimensional and universal wars to reveal their positions and make them depart.

Their directive is to upset our natural order and derail our natural proclivity for good and love.

We cannot see them at work, because they misfire the electrical brain to receive garbled messages. Those who did not call them in will now be set free. Those who did call them in will still have access to their powers of electrical havoc. We are only affected by them through electrical (in human, animal, or inanimate) snafus.

We are unaware of their insinuation into our electrical brain circuitry, because if they were considered part of our way, then it was a defacto invitation to stay. Now they can leave.

Those who called them in were not Earthlings. They have been bred by another interplanetary life form. They will not be comfortable in the Positive System.

Eventually they will depart. They will not tolerate living among contented, rejoicing life.

Leave all conventional thinking aside. There are and were very dark forces here for a very long time.

EXERCISE 19: ASK AGAIN TO BE REWIRED

Ask that you be rewired for the Positive System. Although it is a parable, we do not entirely understand the multidimensional universe. However, you are able to ask for assistance to be rewired. Ask again since you are in a renewed clarity for all of your Highest Good. Some exercises can be done again and again for deepened solidification and service to you and your expansion.

Ask that all those in your life be rewired for the positive system. Trust that as you shift, they will understand what is happening at an unconscious or etheric level; you do not have to explain.

If needed, list again your demands for your Highest Good. Have no judgment on yourself or anyone else. The Positive System means different expression to different people. Revisit what is your Highest Good mentally, emotionally, physically, and spiritually.

Induction to Meditation

Please see page xvii.

Personalize Your Practice

BEGINNER – When you are asking to be rewired for the Positive System, perhaps ask for all those you love as well as the world at large. Send only the highest qualities of the genius of love and light; imagine it any way you conjure. Send those highest qualities of emotional, physical, mental, and spiritual health for ourselves, our loved ones, and Mother Earth.

Perhaps imagine a bolt of white light circling and infusing all of Mother Earth, or any way that works best for you.

MASTER – Those times in our lives when we have been brought to our knees, with time, in hindsight, we can sometimes figure out the gift in the pain. With world events, when horrific, dastardly, destructive times have come, we again try to see if, please, there is sense that can be made, consciousness-raising awareness, and so on.

In our family system, often intertwined so ineffably, the dark or fears were inextricably wired together with love: violence, chaos, deficit, self-doubt, abuse.

Sometimes we are in revolt to giving up the dark, because it was the way we knew love. It is time to know a direct exchange of love to self and other without requiring dynamics and patterns that are of fear. Untangling that weave is to remember that you are Divine, a plural, protected, guided, and connected. Love of self is never overridden or surrendered, but in exquisite mutual exchange through, with, and of the highest qualities of love and light.

There is a soul reason why you have chosen to live on Earth at exactly this time when consciousness was expanding. You have a great deal of Light Work to do.

PARTNER – An at-home partner, if not the partners you are doing this work with, can unconsciously bring home dark energy: disincarnates that get attached to persons or locations, as well as other unwanted debris. Clear sacred space before doing the exercises, and keep clearing your whole home, office, etc. Space blessings, smudging, prayer, and lighting candles are all ways to raise vibration and exorcise undesirable mess.

DATE _____

PLACE _____

TIME _____

WHAT IS MINE TO DO?

Ask the expansive part of yourself.

_____

_____

_____

_____

WHAT IS MINE TO KNOW OR UNDERSTAND THAT I WOULDN'T EVEN KNOW TO ASK?

You are asking your Highest Self to be open to that which you may never have imagined. You are asking to see beyond your customary beliefs, ideas, and construction. Leave room for the possibility of receiving answers in both conventional and unconventional ways.

_____

_____

_____

_____

_____

_____

HOW CAN I LOVE MYSELF BEST RIGHT NOW?

As if you are listening to a friend, stay empty, feel, see, hear, know. If it's more comfortable, close your eyes to receive. Then write whatever comes to you—with no judgment or editing. If you are visual and images come, write what you see. If you hear an internal voice, small or large, write what you hear. If you have thoughts, body sensations, or emotional knowing, take notes. You are chronicling your expansion, a wondrous winding road, a treasure that is all yours.

20

What Is My Purpose?

NOW THAT YOU HAVE finished another inventory of your Highest Good, this is a great time to further explore your mission, purpose, and direction.

Since much has been under revision with respect to your transformation, now it is time to revisit your goals and aspirations. Allow room for great change, but continue self-consulting for sure-footed clarity.

EXERCISE 20: MISSION AND PURPOSE

What is happening?
   Where am I going?
   What is my purpose?
   What is my mission, if different from my purpose?
   May I have a sneak preview of my future?
   Repeating the same questions often leads to new unfolding that wasn't possible until you lived out more transition. Sometimes the repetitive questions give way to understanding in new ways. Trust.

Induction to Meditation

Please see page xvii.

Personalize Your Practice

BEGINNER – As we shift at rapid rates, we often change our values, and what meant so much before gets revitalized with newer meaning.

For instance, take the person who felt money was the answer. He put a piece of paper on his refrigerator to focus on what he was manifesting; however, attainment of the money was not a straight line. Perhaps before he could receive the money, he needed to learn to work well with others, ask for help, hone his self-confidence to feel deserving. So much transformation may have been necessary, that by the time that person has grown, the money is far less of the goal.

Taking a look at your growth from point to point can often assist you determining what is of utmost importance. Enjoy your special journey.

MASTER – "Sure-footed clarity" comes on a spectrum. Sometimes it can be a flash so strong that you know beyond a doubt; other times it could be a process, sometimes coming through systematic prayerful questioning while assessing all angles and potentials.

While in transformation, weigh any big decisions carefully. Know that as your vibration changes, what you attract may not be the ultimate version of what you are working toward. The work of self-expansion is a lifetime process, yes, but in the initial stages we are shifting at rapid rates. Hold holy your commitment to your ultimate goals. Do not give up or give in. Trust in your purpose.

PARTNER – It might be very difficult for a young man with surging testosterone to sit down, look deeply into your eyes, hold your hand, and tell you how he is feeling. Often slowing his system by reaching these meditative states will bring access to information, but sometimes physical action is a necessary complement, like a meditative walk in nature, yoga stretches with breathing, manually manipulating worry beads, drawing images, or any activity that is calming. In time, the more refined energies will be known through both of your personal portals. Keep experimenting to determine what works best for you.

DATE   _____

PLACE   _____

TIME   _____

WHAT IS MINE TO DO?

Ask the expansive part of yourself.

_____

_____

_____

_____

WHAT IS MINE TO KNOW OR UNDERSTAND THAT I WOULDN'T EVEN KNOW TO ASK?

You are asking your Highest Self to be open to that which you may never have imagined. You are asking to see beyond your customary beliefs, ideas,

and construction. Leave room for the possibility of receiving answers in both conventional and unconventional ways.

HOW CAN I LOVE MYSELF BEST RIGHT NOW?

As if you are listening to a friend, stay empty, feel, see, hear, know. If it's more comfortable, close your eyes to receive. Then write whatever comes to you—with no judgment or editing. If you are visual and images come, write what you see. If you hear an internal voice, small or large, write what you hear. If you have thoughts, body sensations, or emotional knowing, take notes. You are chronicling your expansion, a wondrous winding road, a treasure that is all yours.

New World Order of Elevated Consciousness

WE THE PEOPLE of the world have united our mission to explore the oneness of the great Universe. We know that we are held responsible for the magic and the blackness that is ours to control.

Here are the new principles of the New World Order of Elevated Consciousness:

1. Use all resources toward the benefit of all people, animals, and plant growth that will need to live on and perpetuate the ecosystem of our lands and lives.
2. Foresee all interruptions of living to change the manifestos of dark (e.g., there is gratitude for all the light and love).
3. Keep all the debris away so that the next generation will not have to excavate it; find ways to eliminate the refuse now.
4. Listen, for the Earth is talking. Try to welcome the news of the transformation with as much generosity as your newborn children. We have great amounts of acceptance to allow for all the waste that has taken place and has caused our planet to unravel some of its binding truths. Now it is time to see us

as contributors, to welcome the new transformation and enjoy what is to come.

5. All is now of light, so see it as such. Clean your spectacles, get your eyes checked, and no longer question what you see. Let freedom ring, as there is a light that has caught us looking away.

Now it is saying, "We, the Light, are here to inform you. No longer will you not know what is yours to do. Listen to your hearts and act accordingly. We are together and there is much work to accomplish."

(Metaphorically, grab your glove, clean off all baseballs; games will begin in an hour. Jump up and down; games will begin in an hour. Leave the stadiums; the games are in our own backyards. Parents, persons, and animals will frolic together with love, knowing that they are united, for love does abound. See love in all that is you, even if you momentarily disapprove. Turn it into learning to feel the Divine all around. Join hands with strangers and link us all in the family of man to a new world light of loving regard for one another and ourselves at the same time.)

EXERCISE 21: GAMES WILL BEGIN

Feel an internal sense of gratitude for all the light and love, then ask:

What are the ways you can eliminate the refuse in your life now? (Consider recycling or donating unused items to people in need around you).

Close your eyes. Ask Mother Earth what she wants to tell you.

Listen to your heart.

What is yours to do?

Induction to Meditation

Please see page xvii.

Personalize Your Practice

BEGINNER – You, in your corporeal body, are love incarnate. You are so much bigger than you even know, because you are using a linear perception agreement of time, a concrete, visible, tangible, knowable, quantifiable construct of life, along with Life in Life, with many realms of support, expansion, and elevated consciousness guiding. Do it long enough and it becomes the norm.

Once you have put yourself at the service of love and light, you will be guided to know what is yours to do at every moment.

Add play and humor, if you need to, and start small in helping clean up the world mess. Start by cleaning out your garage, basement, and closet, and donating, getting recycling bins, composting, planting, talking to young people about nature, changing company policy where you work to recycle, only hiring vendors that hold those standards as well, cleaning your rivers—just go.

When it comes to you, laugh when you make a perceived mistake. When you scratch the surface, it is always light.

MASTER – The dark is simply un-interpreted light.

As soon as we understand why, it becomes LIGHT.

The zebra that only has three legs gets eaten first by the lion. It wouldn't have survived a stampede, so instead it becomes part of the food chain. Discernment is required to distinguish the circle of life vs. man's inhumanity to man, and man's destruction of Mother Earth. Listening to our Higher Selves is our first act toward Higher Consciousness.

Then go *big* if you dare: return your body, your Mother Earth, and everything else you borrow—the better for it having been gifted to you.

PARTNERS – Have so much joy in cleaning up our planet together.

DATE _____

PLACE _____

TIME _____

WHAT IS MINE TO DO?

Ask the expansive part of yourself.

_____

_____

_____

_____

WHAT IS MINE TO KNOW OR UNDERSTAND THAT I WOULDN'T EVEN KNOW TO ASK?

You are asking your Highest Self to be open to that which you may never have imagined. You are asking to see beyond your customary beliefs, ideas, and construction. Leave room for the possibility of receiving answers in both conventional and unconventional ways.

_____

_____

_____

_____

_____

HOW CAN I LOVE MYSELF BEST RIGHT NOW?

As if you are listening to a friend, stay empty, feel, see, hear, know. If it's more comfortable, close your eyes to receive. Then write whatever comes to you—with no judgment or editing. If you are visual and images come, write what you see. If you hear an internal voice, small or large, write what you hear. If you have thoughts, body sensations, or emotional knowing, take notes. You are chronicling your expansion, a wondrous winding road, a treasure that is all yours.

22

What If

WHAT IS ALL THAT is holy to you, all that is sacred to you, all that encompasses light and divine to you, is the masterful compilation of all that is. It is the space between what has been and what is coming. It is the divine spark of unfurled energy and lessons not yet learned.

What if we could redesign our relationship with the Divine and be an equal? Not as a child asking, but as an age-appropriate request for you.

What if we could come to a more mature acceptance that we must co-create our destiny with a friend who wanted us to attain all that we design for ourselves?

Wouldn't we have to look very carefully at what is ours?

Then "higher power" takes on new meaning. We are ONE. We are ALL. We are the fabric with which we have all that is ours. But what if?

What if we are just as we make ourselves? We eventually come to realize that our thought patterns, our design, are exactly as we wanted all along. Why wait for what Near Death Experiencers call Life Review to see yourself as love?

Because there is no death, there is no judgment for anything you have done. You find self-love from all that you are: expression. So help create all that you are *now*. See yourself as capable of attaining all that you have, and are, and more. See yourself as being the best you. You are a creator; fly high. Rush to make yourself all that you are and see yourself in control. Do not give rise to a down or weaker position. Use your experience to learn what is yours to do.

Seek counsel from advisors here and on alternate planes to give you insight into the glorious partnership we all live. There is no time like the present. Enjoy it all. Sit back and LOVE.

EXERCISE 22: SEEK COUNSEL

Is there a better way to communicate with all the consciousness in all the dimensions and all the beings that are here to help me attain my purpose, my new life, my mission?

What is mine to do in co-creating my new, expanded expression?

Induction to Meditation

Please see page xvii.

Personalize Your Practice

> **BEGINNER** – There hopefully comes a time when you dare become the designer of your own destiny.
>
> From the highest vast power of you, you are designing, not asking. You are in the power seat. Whatever you want, be very clear and very specific, as you are operating from your most expansive reach.
>
> You are infinite in your way of infinite. Never limited.
>
> Some put themselves in a surrender position. There are also great gifts in surrendering to your sense of the Divine or your Highest Self. But be a willing
>
> *(Continued)*

participant in your power. Be of service to your power. Then you are part of the equation. You were given the gift of this lifetime for a very specific reason.

Surrender can include the acceptance of what comes. Unforeseen occurrences may happen, your perceived goals may not be met. The designed goals are often not literal, even though they are your way to live in the most elevated, expansive expression of you in your power. This Earth school is to learn how to give and receive love, but along the way, your designed goals might just help many and few to get there too. Stay steadfast and true to your most powerful you, from your heart, and all else will follow.

MASTER – In receiving intuitive material, there can be static or messages that aren't from the highest qualities of love and light. Ask if this is process. Follow a chain of questioning until messages, feelings, and knowing are elevated and clear once again.

These blips of pushback can either be unwanted energies attracted to your light, or they can be beautiful jewels of process for you to learn more about yourself. Stay centered no matter what is thrown at you. Always feel erect and solid before taking any action. Take the time and have the patience to address static interference through to illumination and grace.

PARTNER – If you are joining over a conference line, or otherwise not in the same physical vicinity, you can still give each other an ethereal hug. (Imagine, conjure, receive.) Sending light, love, and hugs is a beautiful way to connect. You can connect on the physical, through energy, even when you are not physically near each other. You can do it with people living and with those who have passed and often feel "hugged." Enjoy the multidimensional love.

DATE _____

PLACE _____

TIME _____

WHAT IS MINE TO DO?

Ask the expansive part of yourself.

_____

_____

_____

_____

_____

WHAT IS MINE TO KNOW OR UNDERSTAND THAT I WOULDN'T EVEN KNOW TO ASK?

You are asking your Highest Self to be open to that which you may never have imagined. You are asking to see beyond your customary beliefs, ideas, and construction. Leave room for the possibility of receiving answers in both conventional and unconventional ways.

_____

_____

_____

_____

HOW CAN I LOVE MYSELF BEST RIGHT NOW?

As if you are listening to a friend, stay empty, feel, see, hear, know. If it's more comfortable, close your eyes to receive. Then write whatever comes to you—with no judgment or editing. If you are visual and images come, write what you see. If you hear an internal voice, small or large, write what you hear. If you have thoughts, body sensations, or emotional knowing, take notes. You are chronicling your expansion, a wondrous winding road, a treasure that is all yours.

23

Invitation to Death

"DEATH BE NOT PROUD"; have the guts to come knocking. Realize the invitation is not for now, not forever, but for the experience of knowing what exists across the room, behind the door.

See me (Death) as a friend and entreat me. Let me whisper in your ear the secrets.

Let me jostle you into believing that I have it all covered, because I have faith, commitment, and loyalty to that which resides in your domain.

Although I see it not as real, there are levels of disintegration with the loss of dense form. What is my journey? Who comes to help you in transit?

What meaning does one give to one's life? Do I dare ratify all the quick steps leading to nowhere? Undo the repose. See yourself with or without honor.

Sit back and reflect on the quintessential exploration of life in a body.

EXERCISE 23: FACING MY DEATH

The tiniest glimpse of one's death usually gives peace and ease. It helps us face the ultimate unknown and be comfortable with trust for universal support. It also helps us remain unattached to the outcome, as we see our eventual death as a prayer, not of someone unhappy who wants to depart, but as a welcomed friend ready to share the beauty of your life.

Imagine, as with birth, so many wise ones before you who have faced their deaths. See your life in a time line of all that you have lived. Imagine if you were to look at your life in a new way, what new meaning might it bring. Be open for assistance from the divine to guide your writing.

Imagine who might escort you at the time of your crossing. Ask them to let you know of your life so far.

Ask them to let you know what you might want to know right now, in order to better live now and for the future.

What gift is there for me in standing with my death? How might I find peace in knowing that there is no death?

Induction to Meditation

Please see page xvii.

Personalize Your Practice

> **BEGINNER** – If you are not afraid of dying, then you are not afraid to live.
> Elizabeth Kübler-Ross gave one of the first clinical models of death and dying. While bedside to those passing, she noted that the dying patient, often with consciousness or even just out of coma, would speak to that which was not visible in the room. These were often named persons, escorts from

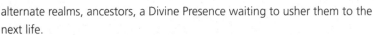

alternate realms, ancestors, a Divine Presence waiting to usher them to the next life.

In a meditative prayer, ask who would come to you on your deathbed in order to feel who you love and who loves you. Make peace with death to better live.

MASTER – Kenneth Ring, by researching people who had flatlined and been revived, substantiated stages of the near-death experience. Ian Stephenson initiated some of the foremost research in reincarnation, across cultures and belief systems. Through many such studies, we understand that our soul is a form without form, which never dies. Like energy, it expands and never ceases, further punctuating that everything is in transition.

To be given an opportunity to be with one who is dying is intimate midwifery that is bestowed with great honor. Of course, utilize all usual and customary medical attention, and please, accompany the passing with your prayers. Use what has worked best for you in cultivating your extrasensory knowing and love. Find the gift in your participation. You have become inextricably linked for precious reasons.

PARTNER – As an extra exercise for partners, and if in meditating it feels correct to do so, share how you would like to die. Be careful to design in self-love. As we co-create our life, so too do we co-create our death.

DATE _____

PLACE _____

TIME _____

WHAT IS MINE TO DO?

Ask the expansive part of yourself.

_____

_____

_____

_____

WHAT IS MINE TO KNOW OR UNDERSTAND THAT I WOULDN'T EVEN KNOW TO ASK?

You are asking your Highest Self to be open to that which you may never have imagined. You are asking to see beyond your customary beliefs, ideas, and construction. Leave room for the possibility of receiving answers in both conventional and unconventional ways.

_____

_____

_____

_____

_____

_____

HOW CAN I LOVE MYSELF BEST RIGHT NOW?

As if you are listening to a friend, stay empty, feel, see, hear, know. If it's more comfortable, close your eyes to receive. Then write whatever comes to you—with no judgment or editing. If you are visual and images come, write what you see. If you hear an internal voice, small or large, write what you hear. If you have thoughts, body sensations, or emotional knowing, take notes. You are chronicling your expansion, a wondrous winding road, a treasure that is all yours.

24

Surrender

UNDERSTAND THAT when we are at our most conscious and curious, those are the times we reckon with our choice to move on to higher or deeper spiritual practice.

This is simple in its own way, yet requires taking on more responsibility and tearing down old structures, like thought forms of what spirituality is or what religion is. How do I make a choice without fear?

Ultimately, by trusting consciousness, you will always choose correctly no matter what is happening with your physical body. We become so open for incredible light to come in.

EXERCISE 24: LETTING THE LIGHT IN

How might I best live in a state of surrender?

How might I take on more responsibility in my spiritual practice?

What do spirituality and religion mean to me?

How might I make choices without fear?

If I could give myself a prayer for surrender and trust, what would it be?

Write your own prayer.

Induction to Meditation

Please see page xvii.

Personalize Your Practice

BEGINNER – "Surrender" will be unique to you. Some might "get" to find the humor. (Buddha said laughter was enlightenment.) Through laughter we begin to understand, without taking it all so personally. Some might "get" to trust and find peace, for the open heart, in the passivity of stillness, is a buoyancy of support.

Then there was the father trying to get his toddler dressed for a play date, only his son would wiggle out of his clothing because he was trying to play. At first the father got frustrated, wanting the baby to be more accommodating. The father was trying so hard to not be late. But then the father laughed, realizing the play date had already begun. The play was with each other. "Surrender" was to the moment, because the moment usually brings everything.

MASTER – There are those who abide blindly, do not question, and live within the borders of acceptability. There are those who question the borders of acceptability, but still abide. And then there are those who rebel against conformity.

In curiosity, in seeking, they question previous ideas to build new roads of knowledge.

Whichever way you choose, do not let your head become so overactive that it gets in the way of your version of surrender. Surrender is an act of the heart, the soul, and all the might of the light.

PARTNER – Share with each other when you are receiving intuitive material, especially when in each other's company.

(Continued)

Twinges, twitches, pangs, high-pitched tones in the ear, crown chakra heat or chills, goosebumps, odors, tightness of throat, visions, and so on. See if there is any meaning meant for the other. You may be a vehicle/messenger for the other. Share.

If enough explanation is not received, if you are not "getting" all the information, ask for the whole message. As though it is a conversation where you heard the words, but you aren't entirely sure what they meant. Ask for more explanation. Keep at active inquiry until you feel solid. You are not impolite. The highest qualities of love and light are generous and patient. If any message comes in with any attitude or disrespect, then it is not the Highest Good.

DATE _____

PLACE _____

TIME _____

WHAT IS MINE TO DO?

Ask the expansive part of yourself.

_____

_____

_____

_____

_____

_____

WHAT IS MINE TO KNOW OR UNDERSTAND THAT I WOULDN'T EVEN KNOW TO ASK?

You are asking your Highest Self to be open to that which you may never have imagined. You are asking to see beyond your customary beliefs, ideas, and construction. Leave room for the possibility of receiving answers in both conventional and unconventional ways.

HOW CAN I LOVE MYSELF BEST RIGHT NOW?

Now, like you are listening to a friend, stay empty, feel, see, hear, know. If it's more comfortable, close your eyes to receive. Then write whatever comes to you—with no judgment or editing. If you are visual and images come, write what you see. If you hear an internal voice, small or large, write what you hear. If you have thoughts, body sensations, or emotional knowing, take notes. You are chronicling your expansion, a wondrous winding road, a treasure that is all yours.

25

Great Defiant Act of Idealism

NOW IS THE TIME to see the change that is in the air. We are all about to face new music. We are breaking the old ways to give way to the new. Here is the way of the peaceful warrior:

1. Open your heart to the freedom of life renewed.
2. See yourself as Divine.
3. Feel into your new existence of life as a friend and welcome adjustment.
4. Join with the many who have seen the many who have come to help.
5. Experience the light as a beacon of remembrance to worlds untouched by human corruption.
6. Enjoy the new ways of love and light.
7. See it all as a new dawn to a new age that we called in.
8. Open the door to each new reveal as though it was a small act of large proportion.

For the time has come to see your face as Divine. Reap the rewards. Help each other find the path to enlightenment, as we are all one and each of us is Divine.

Here now are the many who will bring in the New Resistance. Resist only that which is infused with fear. All else is on the path to enlightenment.

See the light as one would see the bounty before him when he was hungry at a banquet.

Join the chorus of heavenly song. We will overcome the disasters of fear and walk into the light of the new dawn. Open each man's eyes to see the "coming of their (own) Lord" like wonders, for there is no more fear for fear's sake. We will prevail in a new experience of life renewed.

There is nothing to worry about. We have all called this in to become a new frontier to explore, as we have done before.

There have been the Mechanical Age and the Industrial Age. Now is the Age of Multi-Dimensions.

Each will begin to see the light as that which came to free us from our fear. We began to see the protection and guidance that was all of the having. We took our place of rest so that we might become light. Each of us plays a part. There are experiences to have that have *never* been had before. All will have their part to play.

All is entwined to be of grace. See it as a microcosm. As above, so below. What is not tangible in alternate dimensions exists as we do. Laws of physics prevent tangible understanding, yet the many will begin to have tangible experience.

See a new explosion of communication. The path has been lit. Here now are the many who will come forward to speak. Many will see their lives as now having much meaning, as they were waiting to be the ushers to the seats that many will take.

They were the ones who could read the tickets and hold the light. They now understand their purpose. Waiting, waiting, waiting, yet they knew they were waiting for the new dawn.

We are all one.

EXERCISE 25: SEE YOURSELF AS DIVINE

Look in the mirror and say out loud, "I am love" over and over again until you smile with acknowledgment.

Look into your eyes to see into your divinity.

What new ways have protection and guidance been there for me in my life?

Induction to Meditation

Please see page xvii.

Personalize Your Practice

> **BEGINNER** – "As above, so below" means that Heaven can be here on Earth simply by calling all the realms to assist.

> **MASTER** – There are many subtle energies here as friends to help. It may not all be light, but it is love. Love because we are all one, intertwined. Even when wafts of negative energy course through you, know that it is process.
>
> Because you take a pact to live in trust and not fear.
>
> The "gunk" might be due to the fact that we need to be made aware of something, or we could be picking up energies and feelings from people around us that do not belong to us. If you are with strangers, traveling in hotels or airplanes, or hosting a visitor who is depressed or on drugs, you must tell the energies to leave. The people holding these energies are a different matter. Meditate on what is yours to do. No matter what, a boundary is necessary. Only the highest qualities of love and light are allowed in your being, body, home, area, office, and so on.

PARTNER – Healing is the capacity to receive the light. Give each other a healing; send the light from your power grid. Read the energy of your partner before and after.

DATE _____

PLACE _____

TIME _____

WHAT IS MINE TO DO?

Ask the expansive part of yourself.

_____

_____

_____

WHAT IS MINE TO KNOW OR UNDERSTAND THAT I WOULDN'T EVEN KNOW TO ASK?

You are asking your Highest Self to be open to that which you may never have imagined. You are asking to see beyond your customary beliefs, ideas, and construction. Leave room for the possibility of receiving answers in both conventional and unconventional ways.

_____

_____

HOW CAN I LOVE MYSELF BEST RIGHT NOW?

Now, like you are listening to a friend, stay empty, feel, see, hear, know. If it's more comfortable, close your eyes to receive. Then write whatever comes to you—with no judgment or editing. If you are visual and images come, write what you see. If you hear an internal voice, small or large, write what you hear. If you have thoughts, body sensations, or emotional knowing, take notes. You are chronicling your expansion, a wondrous winding road, a treasure that is all yours.

26

You, the All, the Conglomerate

THERE ARE MANY from many different realms that are part of what is about to unfold. What occurs will be for your own benefit always. There are many from different realms that are a part of the events.

There is much riding on this to bring cohesive, collaborative connection to our planet. The beings from different realms will have a stake, as the vibratory high is contagious to their own dimensions that also require elevation.

We, Earth, are the most dense. As we elevate in resolution to conflict, they too reform their methods. We are symbiotic in *all* ways.

There is much affordance to ease and completion. Today will be a great day.

EXERCISE 26: EASE AND COMPLETION

Remember, collect, and gather all the old family and/or cultural beliefs, messages, and adages, spoken or unspoken, around challenges, obstacles, pain, fear, and so forth, then write them down (e.g., "no pain, no gain").

Make a meticulous inventory of each. See if they still work and serve your Highest Self. Honor their place, while putting the defunct ones in the library for reference. Release. Breathe.

Induction to Meditation

Please see page xvii.

Personalize Your Practice

BEGINNER – Where you came from is important to ponder. All the information that shaped you might need to be retired so as to free you from early negative imprinting.

For instance, "where there is a will, there is a way" may require meditation on what is yours to do in each moment. "Completion with ease" refers to everything seemingly falling into place or not feeling like work because it is exactly where you need to be. Your soul knows and it feels correct inside your highest core.

MASTER – Are you completely an Earthling through and through, or did you stare into the night sky wondering what was up there? Do you have any memories of another lifetime? Bleed-through from alternate dimensions? Enjoy it all, if you are one of the lucky ones.

PARTNER – Exchanging old family adages around life should prove to be interesting. Gauge the negativity built into our culture by well-meaning caregivers.

DATE

PLACE

TIME

WHAT IS MINE TO DO?

Ask the expansive part of yourself.

WHAT IS MINE TO KNOW OR UNDERSTAND THAT I WOULDN'T EVEN KNOW TO ASK?

You are asking your Highest Self to be open to that which you may never have imagined. You are asking to see beyond your customary beliefs, ideas, and construction. Leave room for the possibility of receiving answers in both conventional and unconventional ways.

HOW CAN I LOVE MYSELF BEST RIGHT NOW?

Now, like you are listening to a friend, stay empty, feel, see, hear, know. If it's more comfortable, close your eyes to receive. Then write whatever comes to you—with no judgment or editing. If you are visual and images come, write what you see. If you hear an internal voice, small or large, write what you hear. If you have thoughts, body sensations, or emotional knowing, take notes. You are chronicling your expansion, a wondrous winding road, a treasure that is all yours.

27

Bilocation with Those Living in Other Realms

THERE ARE NO WORDS to describe loss. Often it is so devastating, wrenching, and desperate that *no* one may try to define it for you. You alone must make sense of it in any way that works for your beliefs, your faith, or your being. It is yours and yours alone.

Those lifetimes we have lost were as sons, daughters, fathers, mothers, husbands, wives, brothers, sisters, cousins, fathers-in-law, mothers-in-law, uncles, aunts, grandmothers, grandfathers, partners, friends, teachers, business partners, heroes, acquaintances, or were people that impacted your life in immeasurable ways.

Their loss to your life is a gaping hole that will never be filled in quite the same way. Their lives' impact on you is personal and intimate.

One of the first clinical models to explain the process of loss was given by Elisabeth Kübler-Ross, from her work with cancer patients and their families: anger, denial, bargaining, depression, and, finally, acceptance.

Her model was an observance of many, but not all, people's processes.

Be kind and loving to yourself and your loved ones' enduring grief.

Most religions teach not to bother or trouble those souls that have passed through the Earthly realm. Some teach that they have worked on themselves and are finally at peace, or that the deceased may be currently working on themselves to achieve self-love and/or peace, or that they have resisted all invitations toward the light.

We know from accounts over years of research studying near-death experiences (including the work of Dr. Elisabeth Kübler-Ross, Dr. Kenneth Ring, Dr. Bruce Greyson, etc.) that there is an anecdotal understanding that this realm is a school of learning how to give and receive love. The next realms amplify the continued journey.

Through the study of ancient cultures and following reports from children who have reincarnation memories of past lives (from the work of Dr. Ian Stephenson and Dr. Jim Tucker, for example), there is possible, plausible understanding that some of us have more than one Earthly life.

The life you are currently living is not to be squandered; it is a gift to the many lives you touch and a testament to the growth of a soul. The life you mourn, honor, and love also may not be diminished by the act of connecting in an after-death communication.

There are ways that those who have passed over send messages to reach us, through dreams, daydreams, money on the floor, found earrings, two-dollar bills, animals, butterflies, ladybugs, birds, smells like smoke, perfume, sounds, high-pitched tones, tickles in the ear, sharp electrical pangs, chills, goosebumps, hairs on end, extra-electrical charges, unexpected electrical circuitry (e.g., lights, music, television going on and off), refrain of lyrics in your mind playing over and over, objects flying off the shelf, the chains of lockets and necklaces in knots around your neck, unexpected weather, breezes, rainbows, rain, cloud formations, animal messages, angels (either appearances or just felt presences), presents, people who come at exactly the precise moment to give you special messages, and so on.

There are many varied ways to receive messages from other dimensions and realms. We are loved, guarded, and guided. Their spirit lives on in so many ways, both directly and indirectly.

Often what is important to you or what might have been important to the ones who have passed are infusions and inspirations still making their way from memory to our daily life.

If it is accurate that those on the other realms and dimensions are continuing their growth, and if perhaps calling on their assistance is a bother, then here is a possible and comfortable exercise.

EXERCISE 27: BILOCATION TO OTHER REALMS

Send the loved one prayer of the highest qualities of love and light. Feel, think, or imagine yourself bathed in the highest qualities of love and light. Slowing yourself down and raising your vibration allows them to reach you under the very best auspices.

Let them know that you would welcome their visit after they have had their needed time in the light, and only when and if they are ready. Make clear to God and/or guidance to connect only to those who have spent their time in the light, those who have worked on themselves, and those who will only come for your Highest Good.

The Invitation: Close your eyes and conjure their physical form. Walk into their being. Let them know that you would welcome connection. Stay silent and empty.

Trust that whatever you feel is to be honored. If nothing is felt, it may not be appropriate to make the connection. Try again. Make clear your terms of comfort.

Leave room for their timing.

Others who weren't invited to show up may come. It is up to you to converse or not. Send them light.

If it is a biological parent or loved one that you never met, leave room for them to make themselves known. If they were hurtful, harsh, heinous, or neglectful, leave room for an apology. The most important honoring at this moment is to you.

You are inviting them to connect, but *only* if they have worked on themselves and are ready to come for your Highest Good and in love and light.

The Forgiving: See if there were positives that they gave your life, either directly or indirectly. See if some of the greatest assets to your character, ethics, and endurance came, and still come, from some of their influence.

This meditation is a memorial to the beauty of life and our intimate connection with all the souls of our family and our shared human family. They are whispering to us not to fritter away even the briefest second, but to graciously savor the spirit of our highest essence.

They are heroes in death regardless of their role on Earth, and in our eternal expression we are all heroes to be respected.

Try to have dysfunction, hurt, and pain be put aside in favor of love and appreciation outside of time and all ways.

If a charge of electricity, a pang, tears, chills, or any of the previous ways to reach us happens, focus on the area of your body where the sensations are. Inquire of that energy as to who is there and what are they trying to say. This is possibly a time to be poetic and non-linear in your deciphering.

(Keep your notes in order, as this meditation often gets results at the most perfect time, which sometimes is not at the time we ask.)

Induction to Meditation

Please see page xvii.

Personalize Your Practice

BEGINNER – According to Pew Forum, 75 percent of Americans have had spiritually transformative experiences, many of which are after-death communications. After doing the exercise, trust. Answers will come in the perfect time in the perfect way. You are requesting that the consciousness guiding you evolve for your benefit. Give time and patience and trust.

MASTER – This is an exercise in upping the ante, so make clear your need to be in the highest qualities of love and light, the genius of love and light. Make clear for the guidance and love connecting to you to also be of that genius. Stay very open to having the unexpected be downloaded.

PARTNER – It may be best to separate, going into different locations in the house or area. Let each do the exercise with sacred space around them, unless you are both calling on and inviting in the same loved one. Allow for the loved one to answer only one of you at a time. Their relationship and commitment may have been different to each. You might ask if the commitment has been fulfilled in each direction, from you to them and they to you.

DATE

PLACE

TIME

WHAT IS MINE TO DO?
Ask the expansive part of yourself.

WHAT IS MINE TO KNOW OR UNDERSTAND THAT I WOULDN'T EVEN KNOW TO ASK?

You are asking your Highest Self to be open to that which you may never have imagined. You are asking to see beyond your customary beliefs, ideas, and construction. Leave room for the possibility of receiving answers in conventional and unconventional ways.

HOW CAN I LOVE MYSELF BEST RIGHT NOW?

As if you are listening to a friend, stay empty, feel, see, hear, know. If it's more comfortable, close your eyes to receive. Then write whatever comes to you—with no judgment or editing. If you are visual and images come, write what you see. If you hear an internal voice, small or large, write what you hear. If you have thoughts, body sensations, or emotional knowing, take notes. You are chronicling your expansion, a wondrous winding road, a treasure that is all yours.

28

Notes from a Wounded War-Torn Wonderer

WE ARE HERE. If not for you, why would there be anything at all? The gift of love is to be able to see the world in a different way. Each of us can become the new. We will see the beginning of a new dawn and experience our lives as a beginning, not a sorry end.

Try very hard to see yourself as love all the time. Live out loud and do not hesitate to see the beginning of time as a new and exciting venture.

We are with you, so with you. Can you imagine that we are so with you that you are never alone? There are many who see you. Many who live inside you. Many who try to establish the rest of the path as clear. We work overtime and triple-time to be with you and ensure your life is positive.

Until there is worldwide acceptance of the mission, we will endlessly see it through. You have earned this connection. You have called on us day and night.

Not to worry: you are the one to carry this through. We can understand this need to be surrounded by love and light, and we are effectuating this cause.

We are here with the many who are not sure that they can transition to the light. Their regret is so big and so pervasive that they do not see the light. There are those who have a "setup" that wants very much to be with you, ride along, but not do any of the work to remain positive and healthy. Theirs is a ride-along mode that does no good for the greater cause.

We have been hard at work defending the mission and realizing the dream. Yes, we have said that everyone has signed up for the positive system, but it does not mean that they have signed up for the work. Some freeloaders cannot embrace the mission of earnest dedication to positive surrender. We can no longer keep this from you. Please do your magic.

Please say this prayer:

"That which is freeloading, that which is in observation, that which is not in active dedication to the greater good of the Positive System and those parts of me that are still not dedicated to the Positive System, we demand that you/we transmute your resistance to light. There is no room for the indifference of vacillation. Come now, try it on, and hold hands. Be of the light."

EXERCISE 28: EASE AND COMPLETION

Please say this prayer again:

"That which is freeloading, that which is in observation, that which is not in active dedication to the greater good of the Positive System and those parts of me that are still not dedicated to the Positive System, we demand that you/we transmute your resistance to light. There is no room for the indifference of vacillation. Come now, try it on, hold hands. Be of the light."

(Holding fear, anxiety, chaos, or deficit within can keep you back.) Can you try to get a new understanding of self? In active creation, right now, look at all as a positive gift. Be careful not to establish the resistance through your own thoughts. Just simply see yourself as part of the all, and remember: you will never un-know what you already know. Honor where you have come from and where you are going. Honor all who make up the all. See the gifts that all of their lives have been. In this act, you have chosen to go Universal.

Imagine all around you as being a part of that prayer, whether you know them or not. Visualize spreading love and light around the world and into all dimensions, realms, universes, and realities. Invite the all into the gift of love and light. Ask their patterns to expand to the Positive System. See, feel, experience yourself as love and light.

There is great good effectuated today. Be happy all are currently on board. May we all come together in all ways. Joy! Ask again: What might I need to know that I would not even know to ask?

Induction to Meditation

Please see page xvii.

Personalize Your Practice

BEGINNER – The demandment of transmutation from fear to light is one of the most important takeaways from this book. Each time you do not feel your most joy-filled self, please invoke this prayer, as unforeseen freeloading may be going on at your expense.

MASTER – There is competition on the Etheric Realms to guide you, as through your evolution, the consciousness on the etheric so too evolves. Their evolution is more profound from a place of guidance than vicariously. Please pick wisely and hold them to great standards. They must only be of the highest qualities of the genius of love and light for *your* Highest Good. Only then are they allowed to guide you.

PARTNERS – Try an exercise for illumination's sake and ask silently who is guiding your partner. Share only after each has retrieved to the best of their ability. Allow for each to have different ways of communicating with that which guides the other, much less even themselves. See if alternate ways of communication come.

(Once a clock flew off a shelf above a man's head. I asked if his father had loved clocks. Indeed he had. He was making his presence known. Try to leave time to consult with the guide to determine what they were trying to express. Remember though: *always* for *your* Highest Good and of love and light.)

DATE

PLACE

TIME

WHAT IS MINE TO DO?

Ask the expansive part of yourself.

WHAT IS MINE TO KNOW OR UNDERSTAND THAT I WOULDN'T EVEN KNOW TO ASK?

You are asking your Highest Self to be open to that which you may never have imagined. You are asking to see beyond your customary beliefs, ideas,

and construction. Leave room for the possibility of receiving answers in conventional and unconventional ways.

HOW CAN I LOVE MYSELF BEST RIGHT NOW?

As if you are listening to a friend, stay empty, feel, see, hear, know. If it's more comfortable, close your eyes to receive. Then write whatever comes to you—with no judgment or editing. If you are visual and images come, write what you see. If you hear an internal voice, small or large, write what you hear. If you have thoughts, body sensations, or emotional knowing, take notes. You are chronicling your expansion, a wondrous winding road, a treasure that is all yours.

29

Just Look

JUST LOOK ALL AROUND to see the abundance: the sky, the river, the wheat (the staff of life), just there for the taking, and who is there? We are by your side, all of us, to help and teach and follow your wildest dreams.

You have it all and we will be there for this bold, glorious encounter with the new universal energy and love. There is a new world and universal order that will arise, maybe even in your lifetime. It is the burgeoning opening of multidimensional love, a fine-tuning of love and creation to include the Positive System.

We are here for you. Yes, it is right for you to ask what role you play as there are so many involved, all in their own way, adding to the experience of life here on Earth and life in the cosmos.

All effects, the changes in the cosmos, our DNA—you can see it affects all molecular change. We come to find peace within and peace without. There becomes a loving quality to all that is. Smooth and ordered to the growth and longevity. Smooth and ordered to the reproduction.

Just sit back and love.

Just sit back and love. Love all that is and the way it is. We are loving and guiding you. There are many consciousnesses at any time in many individuals. You come to reap the rewards of such a new reality and feel the peace and love all the time. You came to bring a new generation wired for the change.

The DNA shifts when one shifts so dramatically that it can be imprinted from birth.

Imprint the children now. They will know the difference between chaos and peace.

EXERCISE 29: THE ROLE YOU PLAY

Please inquire:

What role do I currently play?

What role will I play in adding to the experience of life here on Earth? To life in the cosmos?

May I have a sneak preview of the evolutionary changes to come?

Induction to Meditation

Please see page xvii.

Personalize Your Practice

BEGINNER – When you make expansions in your patterns of behavior and increase your vibration, reactions are different, trusting is easier, making lemonade out of lemons becomes more attainable. We recover better, with more understanding of why the events were for us to grow from. In the trusting comes more calm. We pass that to all in our intimate circles. Both directly and indirectly, we also help our children better regulate their own emotional and internal states. This resourcing becomes second nature. We evolve.

Trust in your expansion. Trust in your Higher Vibration. Trust in you changing your world for the better.

MASTER – Mark your body changes since beginning the book. See if improvements and unexpected positives have been the result of shifting your DNA. There are many studies on spontaneous remission from disease through guided imagery and hypnosis. You are adding the acceptance of a divine force of healing, adding more light and love to the expanded reach of your vast body.

PARTNERS – After meditating, enjoy an additional exercise. Before sharing what you received as answers, each "go in" on the other. Using your intuitive hearing, seeing, imagining, and thinking, ask what your partner's role might be. See if you possibly enhance the understanding of your role in the world.

DATE _____

PLACE _____

TIME _____

WHAT IS MINE TO DO?

Ask the expansive part of yourself.

_____

_____

_____

_____

_____

_____

WHAT IS MINE TO KNOW OR UNDERSTAND THAT I WOULDN'T EVEN KNOW TO ASK?

You are asking your Highest Self to be open to that which you may never have imagined. You are asking to see beyond your customary beliefs, ideas, and construction. Leave room for the possibility of receiving answers in both conventional and unconventional ways.

HOW CAN I LOVE MYSELF BEST RIGHT NOW?

As if you are listening to a friend, stay empty, feel, see, hear, know. If it's more comfortable, close your eyes to receive. Then write whatever comes to you—with no judgment or editing. If you are visual and images come, write what you see. If you hear an internal voice, small or large, write what you hear. If you have thoughts, body sensations, or emotional knowing, take notes. You are chronicling your expansion, a wondrous winding road, a treasure that is all yours.

30

The Many Who Come

WHEN YOU BEGIN your writing, pangs, pains, electrical charges, high-pitched tones in your ear, smells of smoke or perfume, animal events, and much more may signal that the many have come to help you. Let them know that you are happy to make their acquaintance for your Highest Good.

All is great and on course. There are little incidents along the way, but nothing will derail your spirit or body or mind. Help is here and on the way to realizing your mission.

Just know that all is wonderful and filled with joy. Just enjoy it! Sit back and love. Feel the excitement running through your veins. Yes, nothing will ever be the same. It is all good. Just know that. Listen to the body punctuation. We are addressing your body more and more.

Let's say you make a lunch date with a friend and suddenly find he or she cannot make it. You are sitting alone. You can either choose to storm out and be miffed that you waited for no reason, or you can take yourself out to lunch and enjoy your own company. You just transmuted the negative to a positive.

Take all the chaos, deficit, fear, and anxiety in your life and ask that you now transmute it to inspiration, connection, and co-creation.

Take these words and embed them into you. Now here is the great part: you are not alone.

While you are enjoying your own company, ask what is yours to know that you would not even know to ask. See if your team is there to give you answers or support in your life. Your team is you, your guidance. Who makes up your team? Experts on the other side that you call in.

Life is wonderful. Let it all go and love what you do. There are angels all over you.

We are here to have it go well—very, very well! Just enjoy it all.

We love you,

All of us.

EXERCISE 30: WONDER-FULL

In your wonder, be full of joy and love of self. Go to the beginning of the chapter and read again. Wonder again. Transmute again. You are a constant pump of love, on call at a moment's notice. Enjoy your wonder-full life.

Induction to Meditation

Please see page xvii.

Personalize Your Practice

> **BEGINNER** – How are you "on call" in your life? It's very exciting to see your mission at work. Keep notes.

MASTER – Pumping, breathing in and up, clearing with guided imagery, in whichever way you think, imagine, or feel, use your gifts to transmute the dark to light. As William Arthur Ward said, "If you can imagine it, you can achieve it. If you can dream it, you can become it." You are working at a quantum metaphysical level, so forego practical logic and soar.

PARTNERS – When you are together, sit in the state of wonder: open, curious, and silent. Elevate your prayers through the wonder and then receive, share, and ignite the worlds!

DATE _____

PLACE _____

TIME _____

WHAT IS MINE TO DO?

Ask the expansive part of yourself.

_____

_____

_____

_____

_____

_____

WHAT IS MINE TO KNOW OR UNDERSTAND THAT I WOULDN'T EVEN KNOW TO ASK?

You are asking your Highest Self to be open to that which you may never have imagined. You are asking to see beyond your customary beliefs, ideas, and construction. Leave room for the possibility of receiving answers in both conventional and unconventional ways.

HOW CAN I LOVE MYSELF BEST RIGHT NOW?

Now, like you are listening to a friend, stay empty, feel, see, hear, know. If it's more comfortable, close your eyes to receive. Then write whatever comes to you—with no judgment or editing. If you are visual and images come, write what you see. If you hear an internal voice, small or large, write what you hear. If you have thoughts, body sensations, or emotional knowing, take notes. You are chronicling your expansion, a wondrous winding road, a treasure that is all yours.

31

Big Changes

WOW! Have you told us off! There have been *big* changes since last you wrote. We are with you as an allied force to promote your receiving as well as giving. You are now fully supported to plant seeds and have all.

You are transmitting at great functionality. We are with you in ways and means we could never have guessed. This is greater than all of us could have dreamed. A whole force is coming forward in your honor to announce the coming of your energies. See it all now in your work. Feel it all now in your work.

Human understanding is sometimes reductionist, but the vast comprehension of all of that has occurred is to be openly understood soon. We are working on ways to communicate with you. Your DNA is shifting with purification and strength, all at the same time. You will soon have more endurance and more understanding of your body alignments.

The channelings will come frequently and occur with consistency. If early morning awakenings are in order, there will be pardons for tiredness or reprieve to experience your life without the need for extra sleep.

Your ability to hear high-pitched tones, and to feel and reel in frequencies, will occur rapidly and connectedly to the world's ordered need. You will feel conductions to the electromagnetic fields of wondrous changing worlds. Loosen the reins and see yourself more broadly than you have before.

We will help. Who are we? We are your teammates and advisors about what the world can tolerate on changing frequencies and shifting constructs of thinking, feeling, and living.

There will be disruptions to the expansion of consciousness; we are with you all the while as we come into the new age of multi-dimensional ascension.

No greater time than now has ever occurred to be counted as a barometer of quantifiable understanding. Living it out is essential for continued reporting. The long-lasting effects are just what we are hoping for with your hand at the helm of the results. There is no prediction of the refinement process. Just see the time of "direct" as a time of energies flowing rapidly and assuredly.

EXERCISE 31: WE ARE WITH YOU

How have I balanced my giving to my receiving of love?

How have I become more attuned to alternate-realm energies?

How has my body shifted in acceptance toward a lifestyle of health and sustainability?

How is my hand at the helm of my results? (Look at earlier writing about your purpose.)

What is meant by "the time of direct"? (It is when you can see the perfection in it all.)

Induction to Meditation

Please see page xvii.

Personalize Your Practice

BEGINNER – "Living it out" means that a time of integration of you in relationship to your new energies, of you in your new abilities of sending and receiving, sometime requires what feel like lulls, lags, or limbo, when really you are in integration. This may be a time of putting your new skills to the task of just living it out. Let it all play out in your perfect timing. Stay on course, stay steadfast, and trust. Keep working the work while trusting in the perfection of all.

MASTER – As we come into the new age of multidimensional ascension, you will be called upon to assist the many in attuning to the new revolution of evolution. Stay open to just what is yours to do. You are an instrument of peace within and peace without. Listen to what remarks are made about you, see your impact, and revel.

"Channelings will come frequently and occur with consistency. If early morning awakenings are in order, there will be pardons for tiredness or reprieve to experiences needed." This means that if you awake in the middle of the night, before you return to sleep, ask if there are channelings of only the highest quality of the genius of love and light that need to be received. If yes, go to your journal, computer, iPad and write. Off times in wee hours are often when refined energies can assist. There is no static or interruption. Feel blessed that guidance from your Highest Self has come.

Usually with such a gift, one feels refreshed or can get back to sleep easily.

PARTNERS – Take a moment of stillness together. See if alternate realms, guidance, and your mutual Highest Selves have any information for you. You have the treasured expansion with each to each. Keep a constant check if you are complete in each session; there may be new information trying to get through as one makes an epiphany for the other to experience. The building of each to each is a miracle in and of itself. Watch the unfolding of group in magnificence.

DATE _____

PLACE _____

TIME _____

WHAT IS MINE TO DO?

Ask the expansive part of yourself.

_____

_____

_____

_____

_____

WHAT IS MINE TO KNOW OR UNDERSTAND THAT I WOULDN'T EVEN KNOW TO ASK?

You are asking your Highest Self to be open to that which you may never have imagined. You are asking to see beyond your customary beliefs, ideas, and construction. Leave room for the possibility of receiving answers in both conventional and unconventional ways.

_____

_____

_____

_____

_____

HOW CAN I LOVE MYSELF BEST RIGHT NOW?

As if you are listening to a friend, stay empty, feel, see, hear, know. If it's more comfortable, close your eyes to receive. Then write whatever comes to you—with no judgment or editing. If you are visual and images come, write what you see. If you hear an internal voice, small or large, write what you hear. If you have thoughts, body sensations, or emotional knowing, take notes. You are chronicling your expansion, a wondrous winding road, a treasure that is all yours.

32

Just Because

"JUST BECAUSE" is the best defense for one who wants to accept fully the last laugh.

One who questions can coexist with resistance and life lived open in trust. Both ways are of love.

EXERCISE 32: LIMIT RESISTANCE

What is the difference between "care-full" inquiry to my Highest Self and questions that serve a looping course of resistance? This may be an exercise that is answered as your life plays out, as you begin to engage in self-inventory and/or observation; however, invite in understanding now. Resistance, looping, and perseveration are often defense mechanisms. Inquire about your original wounding that has needed protection. Sometimes the system of defending is so old and so much a part of our pattern that it is difficult to see for ourselves. Ask for guidance as you automatically write.

Induction to Meditation

Please see page xvii.

Personalize Your Practice

BEGINNER – Make certain all answers are from and for your Highest Good. If answers or feelings hold any kind of negative energy, keep requesting to become more elevated in expression, as well as sending and receiving.

Constant checks through body scanning and listening in new ways can make more apparent your elevated expansion. Constantly energetically "sweep" or "clear" your home/area and body before inquiry takes place. Review the way you are asking the question and see whether perseveration of the same issues need to be approached from different vantage points. Keep asking for elevation. A spiritual intervention is often the best antidote for breaking cycles of rigidity, looping, and/or perseveration.

MASTER – Recalibration of thinking may be needed at this time. See if any residual old patterns need to be addressed. Inquire for constant self-inventory. As one layer loosens, new layers come into view. Self-inquiry for maximum expansion and elevation is an ever-growing, always needed process, forever and ever.

PARTNER – What does "just because" mean to the two of you? How do you rub up against each other and bother each other? See if there aren't still places of you that mirror those infractions. See if you aren't up for a realignment for your own good. The places that upset us most are unforgiven aspects of self, even if not exactly a mirror. Look for the poetry.

DATE

PLACE

TIME

WHAT IS MINE TO DO?

Ask the expansive part of yourself.

WHAT IS MINE TO KNOW OR UNDERSTAND THAT I WOULDN'T EVEN KNOW TO ASK?

You are asking your Highest Self to be open to that which you may never have imagined. You are asking to see beyond your customary beliefs, ideas, and construction. Leave room for the possibility of receiving answers in both conventional and unconventional ways.

HOW CAN I LOVE MYSELF BEST RIGHT NOW?

As if you are listening to a friend, stay empty, feel, see, hear, know. If it's more comfortable, close your eyes to receive. Then write whatever comes to you—with no judgment or editing. If you are visual and images come, write what you see. If you hear an internal voice, small or large, write what you hear. If you have thoughts, body sensations, or emotional knowing, take notes. You are chronicling your expansion, a wondrous winding road, a treasure that is all yours.

33

Reprieves from the Unity

YOU HAVE BEEN CHOSEN to see the worlds as one. You have been experiencing the energies, gifts, and releases of all. There are certain reprieves from the unity that have cost you a feeling of being untethered. Do not worry.

Remember: there is pain, but no fear. Please remember "no fear." We have tried as best as we can to prepare your body for the experiences of the new results. There are costs to the transference of light and love.

We are blowing open the circuitry of old patterns, replacing them with a new result.

You are totally of the light. There are no wrinkles. You will see reward soon.

Remember there was great anxiety? All gone. Remember there were fine reasons for dwelling on hurts that you fumed about? Now you review, but take it all to the highest ground.

You are being further reworked to absorb energies not of your understanding or experience. There are many results that have not yet been reached. Listen to the many who know how to help.

Some words will seem out of place and will hold a vibration that can render little meaning for you. Your brain is being designed for alternate grasp.

Usual and customary recall has eluded you. Let it be. Let us help. We are the many from different worlds that came to assist the transformation of the New Age. The Age of Light and Love is the beginning of love of self and other at the same time.

There is a different sensibility for the occurrences of now. People's hearts have been opened and light is seeping in.

Catastrophes are assisting. Painful transformation is helping. We are choosing people to usher in the New Worlds here: people, like yourself, who can see the needs of light and love. Listen to your heart and understand that we are here for the greater good. So are you. See yourself as a loving conduit for the energies that will be filled.

Your purpose is to help us be in advance of knowledge and reason, loving and forgiveness, seeking and wonderment. Eventually new methodologies will occur, so that there is a feeling of acceptance and love everywhere. Nation will help nation. Earth will breathe clean air again. Soil will birth bounty. Animals will see themselves as joyous contributors to the cycle of life.

Many galaxies are involved, and many experiences of result are coming forward.

Listen to your heart and guidance. Become one with all that is Divine. Be of the light—the highest ground is grace. The idea of the work is to find the loving regard in every situation. Just stay calm in breath and thought. You are the one who called us in. We are you. Every minute you are to feel us as one. Love. Love. Love.

Many have called on us. The Earth and people were sicker and upsetting the evolutionary continuance. Mutations were around in rapid event. Now there will be a reversal of all that is disturbing Earth. Energies and fields of health, result, and reward are already here.

Babies will not hold the genetic patterns of their ancestors. We will open ourselves to less and less disease. Families will stay together and not endure harsh splintering.

Plants will override the dirty air and take a big hit for our misuse of the Earth.

Animals will soon be treated with exaltation. Our ocean life will cry out louder and be helped. The plastic islands will see the transformation of recycle. Big corporations will go in and have industrial facilities refurbish waste use. New plastic will not be used.

The Earth is no longer crying but speaking words of "how." People will hear the call. The symbiotic harmonies are singing. Now that you have called us in, hang in there, for the stage is set. We are working the energies to entice, not repel.

Soon there will be a worldwide holding of the new; the family of man is coming forward with the result. We have all been here. You saw the crossroads. Yes, life and consciousness are eternal. But you saw the ability for it all to shift right now. You are love and light. Be of solid wonderment, not fear-based review or query.

EXERCISE 33: THE GRACE OF HIGHEST GROUND

What have been my costs in the transference to love and light?

How has my pain not included fear? (Sometimes we have to be in so much pain, and so hate where we are at, that we override the fear to make the change. Flexing new muscles, shifting worldviews, and breaking down old patterns requires a support system.)

Write about where/how you are being reinforced: By your own resilience? Through others? Where else?

How does my taking a beat, a pause, for consulting with all that is my divine guidance, help find the Highest Ground?

Induction to Meditation

Please see page xvii.

Personalize Your Practice

BEGINNER – "Costs" might be the way you aren't who you used to be, but the pluses outweigh the minuses. See if your new way of being is the gift you have been praying for. Have your prayers been answered?

MASTER – You are the one who called in the new age of expanded light. Why were you born at exactly this time? Why have you chosen to work toward the greater goodness of self and other?

PARTNER – "The Earth is no longer crying, but asking how." Ask each to each just how we have begun to help Mother Earth recently. See if new commitments can be made for your union to help each other, the children, the animals, and Mother Earth.

DATE _____

PLACE _____

TIME _____

WHAT IS MINE TO DO?

Ask the expansive part of yourself.

_____

_____

_____

_____

WHAT IS MINE TO KNOW OR UNDERSTAND THAT I WOULDN'T EVEN KNOW TO ASK?

You are asking your most high self to be open to that which you may never have imagined. You are asking to see beyond your customary beliefs, ideas, and construction. Leave room for the possibility of receiving answers in conventional and unconventional ways.

_____

_____

_____

_____

_____

HOW CAN I LOVE MYSELF BEST RIGHT NOW?

Now, like you are listening to a friend, stay empty, feel, see, hear, know. If it's more comfortable, close your eyes to receive. Then write whatever comes to you—with no judgment or editing. If you are visual and images come, write what you see. If you hear an internal voice, small or large, write what you hear. If you have thoughts, body sensations, or emotional knowing, take notes. You are chronicling your expansion, a wondrous winding road, a treasure that is all yours.

34

No Dying

NATURAL ORDER is perfection, no matter how it goes down. Live of that. Revel in and love your body. Your days will be filled with great love and advanced emotional understanding of forgiveness.

You will feel detached, but it is because you see the perfection and do not linger in the loss. All is still here for you. You play with that of the unseen realms readily. There is no loss for you.

Each is here, but no one wants you to pass up an opportunity to work directly with the Divine. Divine is an ALL of unfathomable proportion and grace. We are all here, but we want you to feel guided by a newer concept of Divine as you know it, and a newer expanse of result. We love to assist and transform, to create, co-create, remark, and rejoice.

We love to join and fill you with loving and unknown exaltation. Day by day there will be newer understanding. Day by day new events and meanings will occur. Trust that when one is with you, one is held in the orbit of the new.

Soon all will join, assist, transform, create, co-create, remark, and rejoice. Soon we will all be of one mission and method: love of self and other at the same time.

Sometimes your life is not long. Just trust that your body is a beautiful vehicle for the energies that make you a messenger. Your energies may change as we need your vehicle. Your original consciousness is with you but blended with the all.

There is bounty beyond description. Just know that you are of exquisite and refined reach, soon to entice, not repel as foreign.

Animals may be changing their reactions to you. Your pets are being rewired as we speak. Their sleep patterns will change. There will be differences in personality. We are with them. Animals are being worked with and on their way.

So much is coursing through your body that we are fine-tuning the chords of emotion. Leave it to us for now. We are with you.

Your readings of consciousness will happen in different and bigger ways. It is all good. The All will communicate anew. You will feel it all uniquely, out of order to the past occurrences.

EXERCISE 34: YOU ARE BLENDED WITH THE ALL

Have I had more after-death or alternate-realm communication lately, since I started these exercises?

Am I congruent with perfection in everything, no matter how it seemingly plays out? Is that my way of forgiving?

Have I noticed a detachment in my experience of loss? Is it linked to my communications with the unseen realms?

Do I trust that when I hold new frequencies within my being, others are held in the orbit of love and light?

Induction to Meditation

Please see page xvii.

Personalize Your Practice

BEGINNER – Are you aware of changes in your receiving that make it new and different to the ways you knew before? Look for exciting and varied experiences of synchronicity.

MASTER – The feeling of detachment or neutrality is a mastery of nothing as lost. All consciousness is available for us at the perfect moment of illumination. Review times, places, and reactions. See if there has not been positive acceptance toward loss.

PARTNER – Loss can be as small as not showing up for the session with your partner, or as monumental as earthly demise. Review with your partner the times of loss experienced with each other and just how you processed through those feelings toward connection again.

DATE _____

PLACE _____

TIME _____

WHAT IS MINE TO DO?

Ask the expansive part of yourself.

_____

_____

_____

_____

WHAT IS MINE TO KNOW OR UNDERSTAND THAT I WOULDN'T EVEN KNOW TO ASK?

You are asking your Highest Self to be open to that which you may never have imagined. You are asking to see beyond your customary beliefs, ideas, and construction. Leave room for the possibility of receiving answers in conventional and unconventional ways.

_____

_____

_____

_____

HOW CAN I LOVE MYSELF BEST RIGHT NOW?

As if you are listening to a friend, stay empty, feel, see, hear, know. If it's more comfortable, close your eyes to receive. Then write whatever comes to you—with no judgment or editing. If you are visual and images come, write what you see. If you hear an internal voice, small or large, write what you hear. If you have thoughts, body sensations, or emotional knowing, take notes. You are chronicling your expansion, a wondrous winding road, a treasure that is all yours.

_____

_____

_____

_____

35

In Unison

EACH NEW DAY contains many dimensions and many lives in multiple time zones. You are about to observe many lives in many lives—life in life.

When one asks the existential dilemma of "what is mine to do?" one asks for all expressions and all times. Not to complicate matters, but we even have multiple expressions in each dimension; therefore, when others are speaking to you and you to them, there are many of you and many of them.

These are effortless efforts that come because we are all connected to the force of healing that exists for all in the all.

What if we only had the one stream of video that referenced our existence? What if we believed that this was all there is? Of course there would be stiff competition for all that there was as a finite amount to attain. Lo, we are not *finite*. We have so much more that we do not see, that which is unseen, yet does exist. There are so many levels, layers, and lessons that we will easily express it all in terms we can understand and grasp. Where, who, and how are we?

Long ago, time and place lost existential meaning. New nations arrived from worlds concordant with ours. We began to express in sophisticated organizational pods. We grouped in advancement. We survived in coordination and readjusted to the many who held up a sign for connection.

Recent marches for the betterment of humanity came on the heels of new regard for the many who lead lives that are aided, supported, and advised by realms they cannot quite detect.

All that is alternate living requires an expression of non-linear and non-specific connections to those groups of consciousness that do not see, think, feel, and hear quite like we do.

Accomplishments are gauged and recused when there is open elicitation to garner and reap for the holder of the reference. Keep trying and trust; get in the flow and it will begin to emerge.

There are pockets of love so deep and fulfilling when time seems to stop and perceptions are richer. You can fall into those deep sovereign moments and believe that this is because there are strong feelings for those you are with. No, there are strong feelings, but there are the many who are a part of that council who make themselves known only through energetic reference. We are the ones who fall short in the interpretation. We fall short because we are limiting our reference ability as well as our ability to see. We cannot hear, think, or report as real unless we conspire to exclude this reasoning.

Let us open our hearts and "see" in a new way. Adjust the ones who are limited to feel themselves in a group even if they only see, feel, and hear one. Many are around all the time. Many are in service to your earth-flesh expression. Many are involved in the events of our planet.

You ask, "If that is so, how could we be in such dire straits?" Because sometimes, as with a slingshot, we have to pull the rubber band far backward to accomplish, aim, and hit. We have been pulled elastically back in limited perception, all in an effort to be opened wider, wider, wider. You ask, "Do we understand?" No, we are just beginning to make ourselves known.

Love is the all, but with a refined objective to give "all" a meaning of kindness, regard, and ease. Love is the wanted assistance that everyone is beginning to pray for. Most of this limited realm is ready to be opened.

You ask, "Why was this perception shut off in the first place?"

Perception was not shut off. Perception was not utilized for the benefit of mankind, the planet, and beyond. Once we fantasize in unison about another reality not including war, poverty, or pollution—that is, one of sustenance—we create it. Energies are creating and beginning to levitate. Openings are being revealed to the masses that require interpretations. Listen to our words and feel us in our/your hearts. We are one.

EXERCISE 35: PERCEPTION NOW UTILIZED

If in fact my perception was not "shut off," but just not used for the benefit of mankind, planet, and beyond, what might I imagine the gifts of a new world to be?

I am in creation of a group fantasy for another reality that does not include war, poverty, and pollution. We will in unison create a new revolution of evolution. In this I pray.

Induction to Meditation

Please see page xvii.

Personalize Your Practice

> **BEGINNER** – Once you begin in prayer, to no longer resist, no more disparaging Pollyanna-ish derision is allowed. Go boldly without looking back. Believe and begin to be of love in every deed and thought.

> **MASTER** – The group soul of consciousness will provide the how; just show up in the goodness for all as one readied to be of grace, now and forevermore.

PARTNER – Think of when in your relationship your perception might have been shut off for your own benefit, much like a surprise party has clues that are not seen for the benefit of the recipient's joy. Try to forgive what could not have been known, and embrace the timing as perfect.

DATE _____

PLACE _____

TIME _____

WHAT IS MINE TO DO?

Ask the expansive part of yourself.

_____

_____

_____

_____

_____

_____

_____

WHAT IS MINE TO KNOW OR UNDERSTAND THAT I WOULDN'T EVEN KNOW TO ASK?

You are asking your Highest Self to be open to that which you may never have imagined. You are asking to see beyond your customary beliefs, ideas,

and construction. Leave room for the possibility of receiving answers in both conventional and unconventional ways.

HOW CAN I LOVE MYSELF BEST RIGHT NOW?

Now, like you are listening to a friend, stay empty, feel, see, hear, know. If it's more comfortable, close your eyes to receive. Then write whatever comes to you—with no judgment or editing. If you are visual and images come, write what you see. If you hear an internal voice, small or large, write what you hear. If you have thoughts, body sensations, or emotional knowing, take notes. You are chronicling your expansion, a wondrous winding road, a treasure that is all yours.

36

Why Are We...?

DEAR GENIUS of Light and Love,
Why are we so exhausted from trying to be better people and deserving of rewards?

Why are we so exhausted from depleting results that leave us without all efforts renewed? Why are we extinguished from the fires that were burning inside our immense passions? When did everything go straight to hell? Who are we? Who are the ones that can lead us anew? Where is the bounty? And why do we fail?

Just as there is a new sunrise every day, just as there is a new round of birds chirping, rest assured that there is also change within the broader experience of sameness.

Each individual is exhausted and in need of rest and reward. There have been difficult energies here that have caused a reaction of harm and destruction. We are here now, the energies that will assist in reversing difficulty, catastrophe, and famine.

Listen to the new call to action. Listen to the new attempts to reverse the destruction and see everyone's part to play in a "reap mode."

But the calls must be heard; the clarion call of love and light will prevail and continue. Be not of the dark: chaos, confusion, and fear.

Be not stalwart in continuance of the old destructive patterns of fear-based action and thinking. Be not difficult, judging, unreasonable, and dispassionate.

Lo, these times will soon be behind us, and events will come forward to expose the multi-dimensions that will aid, assist, and employ the unity of the worlds. We have always been one, but fears clouded all the calls to unite. There is now the ability to see forward to the unity of all the worlds. Yes, we are here and we are one.

EXERCISE 36: LISTEN TO THE NEW CALL TO ACTION

What are your new attempts to reverse destruction? (Remember to get all answers from your Highest Self.)

How/when have you been feeling a sense of oneness?

Do you sense an internal calling toward peace?

Induction to Meditation

Please see page xvii.

Personalize Your Practice

> **BEGINNER** – Review old self-destructive habits that might have fallen by the wayside. What do you imagine/think/feel might have been the cause?

> **MASTER** – Stay "local" with you personally. Try to not get caught in the arguments about the global, for now. With each new beginning of expansive elevation, we inspire the group at large. Consult with your Highest Self for your timing to be of service to others.

> **PARTNER** – What is your part to play for the mutuality of the partnership?

DATE _____

PLACE _____

TIME _____

WHAT IS MINE TO DO?

Ask the expansive part of yourself.

_____

_____

_____

_____

WHAT IS MINE TO KNOW OR UNDERSTAND THAT I WOULDN'T EVEN KNOW TO ASK?

You are asking your Highest Self to be open to that which you may never have imagined. You are asking to see beyond your customary beliefs, ideas, and construction. Leave room for the possibility of receiving answers in both conventional and unconventional ways.

_____

_____

_____

_____

_____

_____

HOW CAN I LOVE MYSELF BEST RIGHT NOW?

*As if you are listening to a friend, stay empty, feel, see, hear, know. If it's
more comfortable, close your eyes to receive. Then write whatever comes to
you—with no judgment or editing. If you are visual and images come,
write what you see. If you hear an internal voice, small or large, write
what you hear. If you have thoughts, body sensations, or emotional knowing, take notes. You are chronicling your expansion, a wondrous winding
road, a treasure that is all yours.*

Part 3

THE TREE OF LIFE

Unity

37

State of Rapid Transformation

*D*EAR GENIUS of Light and Love,
How are we to be understood by all the beings and consciousnesses that will partake in the expansion if there are different frequencies and energies? How will it all go down?

We are in a state of rapid transformation. When those of you who reap the reward of an open heart come together, you will soon begin to see the dimensions of the all. It will be a group unfolding so as not to scare or prevent an unfolding of differences. We are all lined up to slowly, effectively be there for all who have an open heart.

Listen to each one's cues. Listen to the group's call. Listen to the factual overlays that begin to fall by the wayside when those of you who come together begin to see events as an effortless effort to expose the dimensions of the beyond.

"Beyond" is the consciousness that surrounds and is in the all. All is the consciousness, and pockets of concentrated consciousness that are here for you and the worlds.

Live as though all is normal. Live to aspire toward an open heart, so as to accept that which may be outside normal. Live so that we are all one. Yes, there may be events that will be Earth-shaking, and yes, there will be events that will open all the ones to their original states of love, ecstasy, and all-knowing. Open hearts will feel sturdier in their thinking and their feeling. We will explore dreams and prophecy. We will have awakenings with you, where ideas are not discarded.

There will be no more group collusion to disregard all that is here. We operate in different dimensions at all times to a larger result than one can imagine or fathom. We know that this changes a great deal, and that life will never be the way it was.

Understanding for the benefit of all will reassure those who already know not to feel alone or crazy. Each person will report to the other, and most events will occur so that there is comfort and love.

The events will appear slowly and pervasively. We will be together in ways never experienced before, but all will be smooth and loving. The wondrous events will fill everyone's hearts and minds.

The children will be aware first. They are already close to the events that will occur. They are in on it, as before they were born into the dense expression of a body, they planned for all that would result. Here they are now to assist in the transformation. We are all very excited for you. You just do not know it yet.

EXERCISE 37: EFFORTLESS EFFORT

Is my heart wide open? If not, may I integrate all that needs honoring and bring down my last remaining defenses?

May I please have a palpable understanding of my connection to the all?

May I please feel/see/know the light of the children, here to bring us the future in ways we cannot yet fathom?

Am I free of group collusion to disregard all that is here?

What might I now be able to fathom that I was not able to see before?

Induction to Meditation

Please see page xvii

Personalize Your Practice

BEGINNER – "Group collusion" is, at a quantum physical level, a group manifestation of assigned and agreed-upon beliefs. The group beliefs can easily be undone, as each heart opens to reshape each new worldview in total trust. Total trust doesn't mean being open and vulnerable to all. It means to go up and in, to meditate, feel, and know from your deepest core and from your Highest Self that each movement, action, and thought is congruent with your open heart. Knowing exactly what is yours to do from an open heart is all that is asked.

MASTER – Integrating all that needs honoring before shedding your defenses requires an allowance for all parts of self, psyche, and emotions to be held in gratitude, for all of you has served you well to this point. The integral part of the self never wants to feel as though it is dying or leaving. So we honor the job all parts of you have done to date. We rejoice in you being you. Now it is time to ask all parts of self, psyche, and emotions to trust in the expansion. In the act of "going universal," in the request to see the oneness, we see the love and we help ourselves forge through to Higher Vibrational Expansion and no longer operate from old patterns that held us in fear. As a symbiotic system we are interconnected, and sometimes just one awareness can trigger a great transformation.

It may feel as though you have done this before, but you cannot revisit this enough. You are an ever-changing, in-creation soul of vast proportion. Expansion is recalibrated regularly.

PARTNER – Just check whether there is any group collusion between parties. If working with a romantic partner, inquire in meditative state together. If in a book club, or meeting-style group, break up into dyads and revisit your feelings about group collusion. See if sharing with the group at large can be done for beneficial result, as one awareness can sometimes trigger a group transformation.

DATE _____

PLACE _____

TIME _____

WHAT IS MINE TO DO?

Ask the expansive part of yourself.

_____

_____

_____

_____

_____

_____

WHAT IS MINE TO KNOW OR UNDERSTAND THAT I WOULDN'T EVEN KNOW TO ASK?

You are asking your Highest Self to be open to that which you may never have imagined. You are asking to see beyond your customary beliefs, ideas,

and construction. Leave room for the possibility of receiving answers in both conventional and unconventional ways.

HOW CAN I LOVE MYSELF BEST RIGHT NOW?

As if you are listening to a friend, stay empty, feel, see, hear, know. If it's more comfortable, close your eyes to receive. Then write whatever comes to you—with no judgment or editing. If you are visual and images come, write what you see. If you hear an internal voice, small or large, write what you hear. If you have thoughts, body sensations, or emotional knowing, take notes. You are chronicling your expansion, a wondrous winding road, a treasure that is all yours.

38

Angels

DEAR ONE,

We have been thinking that there are no angels here on Earth. We believe that all angels are here in Heaven. Do you feel that way?

Dear Divine,

No, I rather thought that there *were* angels here on Earth. You see, I have thought many to be at the right place at the right time in assistance to others that helped shape a life in the right direction. Is that not an angel?

Dear One,

Okay, so if this is your definition of an angel, then the many will now become angels. The many will now be at the right place at the right time so as to effect a new course. This new course is the supreme allowance of all to experience a knowing of light and love. How amazing will that be, for all of mankind to experience love and light at the same time just because everyone decided to feel safe enough to open their hearts and rest easy that that was okay? We are at a crossroads where everyone is here in this dimension at the same time, hoping that life holds more.

EXERCISE 38: LIFE HOLDS MORE

Have I had my supreme experience of love and light?

Have I been at the right place at the exact right time to help shape another's life in the right direction?

What is my belief around "being at the right place at the right time"?

Often those moments of life-changing, course-correcting inspiration are appreciated but aren't pondered for the exquisite intricacies that needed to be in place for all to have happened. Take a moment and make a time line of these events. Appreciate the exquisiteness on your behalf.

Induction to Meditation

Please see page xvii.

Personalize Your Practice

BEGINNER – Are there any spiritually transformative experiences that have changed your or a loved one's life? Feel, think, and imagine how that shifted you until now. What is your definition of an angel?

MASTER – List all the times you were aware you said or did the exact right thing at the exact right time for another. Ask from a meditative state, "Were there more?" See if the answer serves to open you even more. Are you an angel? (Ask from your Highest Self, not your head.)

PARTNER – Is there any time both of you can remember being there for each other at exactly the right time? How did it change your life? Or how would your life have changed if it *had not* happened? Both are valid. Share.

DATE _____

PLACE _____

TIME _____

WHAT IS MINE TO DO?

Ask the expansive part of yourself.

_____

_____

_____

_____

_____

_____

_____

WHAT IS MINE TO KNOW OR UNDERSTAND THAT I WOULDN'T EVEN KNOW TO ASK?

You are asking your Highest Self to be open to that which you may never have imagined. You are asking to see beyond your customary beliefs, ideas,

and construction. Leave room for the possibility of receiving answers in both conventional and unconventional ways.

HOW CAN I LOVE MYSELF BEST RIGHT NOW?

Now, like you are listening to a friend, stay empty, feel, see, hear, know. If it's more comfortable, close your eyes to receive. Then write whatever comes to you—with no judgment or editing. If you are visual and images come, write what you see. If you hear an internal voice, small or large, write what you hear. If you have thoughts, body sensations, or emotional knowing, take notes. You are chronicling your expansion, a wondrous winding road, a treasure that is all yours.

39

Stop!

HOW AM I to understand just what is mine to do?

How are we, as a nation of humanity and conscious-ness, supposed to understand what is ours to do?

Where are we headed?

Are there enough resources if we all band together from this moment forward?

Will there be innovation to forge other avenues to success for all the living to reach optimum health? Will we want for anything?

Will we regress/progress to alternate land-orientation cultures that require no irrigation or corrective measures to simplify the opportunity to thrive?

How are we to advance and still unharm all that we have? Where are there enough resources, people, and knowledge to see it all through to a logical end?

Is the end of life as we know it here?

Are we to regroup, reshape, and return to the unfortunate means that we were operating from even in the face of the ultimate demise of cattle, land, and human consciousness?

Where are we in the grand scheme of time and effort? Help us. STOP!

Enough questions. Rest assured that consciousness will remain eternal, and here is not just here. This means that time and place are irrelevant to the constructs under which you are asking, as we are everywhere all at the same time.

Time is a quadrant of measure, nothing more. Time exists for all as a unified field of reason that repeats in our thoughts and in our living (déjà vu). Time is an alternate, linear connection to place and reason. Nothing more.

We are together, yet separate, all at the same time. We are all one, yet sovereign, all at the same moment. We are of constant motion and perceive standstill, yet we are moving at warp speed. Much of who we are and what we are alternately exists in different times and places. We are multidimensional.

Let this drumroll start, let this clarinet begin the smooth, sultry, steamy riff that will permeate brains and emblazon itself into memorable context.

We are multidimensional and have been since we began!

We try to construct alternate meaning to forget: we are all one.

The universe in its vast, infinite, ineffable expression is all one. We jump at a consciousness's rate of jump to experience all the all in no time.

Let me repeat this all in another way: We are one and have been, all ways and always. We can infiltrate each other's bodies, thoughts, and hearts, not just here but in all the universes.

Here we are, yet you are at this moment hooked into universal flow as though we were one. Let that be the mission of all who live here on Earth, as an undoing of the collusion when each signed up to remember the Earth times together. Now there is no more need for that occurrence. We are one. Divine is all and all is Divine. Just relax into the reveal and ponder gently. More will be forthcoming.

Love to all of you,

The Divine

EXERCISE 39: BILOCATION WITH THE LIVING

As an exercise, pick a living Earth being you want to connect with, but this time we are not going to use conventional methods. Close your eyes and imagine that person in front of you. Walk into that being and ask his or her Highest Self a question. Wait for an answer.

The answer may come in many ways, such as a knowing, a feeling, or a thought. If there is no response, ask permission from that being's Highest Self to know why you are being blocked.

Stay unattached to outcome, and trust. There may be information that comes through from the being's Highest Self that gives you an entirely different aspect to what and how he/she might communicate. Remember this communication is in mutuality to the all.

Sometimes the all has a sense of humor. Sometimes there is a process involved for you to grow. Ask if that is the case, and then do the process as your Highest Self suggests. Trust.

Induction to Meditation

Please see page xvii.

Personalize Your Practice

BEGINNER – Remember, when you begin this exercise, to surround yourself, your body, and your area of sacred meditation with only the highest qualities of the supreme genius of love and light. That way you will not be able to go anywhere or be with anyone who is not in mutuality to the highest calling of love and light.

MASTER – If you are not getting any response, are being blocked or stymied, please try using an emissary of the highest qualities of the genius of love and light to make the connection for you. That can be a choice of your sense of the Divine that is personal for you. You can meditate on just who that might be for you. Some ideas: Buddha, Consciousness, God, Jesus, Archangel Michael, Lakshmi, Mohammed the Prophet, High Consciousness, ancestors, masters, sages that are your guides, and so on.

PARTNER – This is a time for you to do this exercise with each other. You have been asked to do this before. This time, set a series of questions that appeal to you both and enter with love. Test out the answers with the other. See if the feeling of entry has any quality to it. Make certain the setting is sacred and of the highest qualities of the genius of love and light before progressing. This exercise is only for the Highest Good of all.

DATE _____

PLACE _____

TIME _____

WHAT IS MINE TO DO?

Ask the expansive part of yourself.

_____

_____

_____

_____

WHAT IS MINE TO KNOW OR UNDERSTAND THAT I WOULDN'T EVEN KNOW TO ASK?

You are asking your Highest Self to be open to that which you may never have imagined. You are asking to see beyond your customary beliefs, ideas, and construction. Leave room for the possibility of receiving answers in both conventional and unconventional ways.

_____

_____

_____

_____

HOW CAN I LOVE MYSELF BEST RIGHT NOW?

As if you are listening to a friend, stay empty, feel, see, hear, know. If it's more comfortable, close your eyes to receive. Then write whatever comes to you—with no judgment or editing. If you are visual and images come, write what you see. If you hear an internal voice, small or large, write what you hear. If you have thoughts, body sensations, or emotional knowing, take notes. You are chronicling your expansion, a wondrous winding road, a treasure that is all yours.

_____

_____

_____

_____

40

The End Game

DEAR ONES,

I am you. I am of the Earth. I walk as you. I talk seldom. Here is the context.

Just as there are many of the light, there are the many who reside in the darkness of fear. We walk in our shoes with the knowing that we were to draw our expressions to a logical conclusion: no more fear. Here we are of the Earth and filled with a transcendence of love. Here we are and here it will end. Please see yourselves as the endgame of all that came before. Just as there were useful times adjusting to the reveal, now we are the light. All is love and we are love.

EXERCISE 40: TRANSCENDENCE OF LOVE

What is my process to integrate today?

May I live in the transcendence of love as a perpetual request, so that I may raise my vibration of loving regard for myself and all that is for me in my life?

May I quickly "see" that which is not for me to do?

And find the loving regard in growth and process?

Induction to Meditation

Please see page xvii.

Personalize Your Practice

BEGINNER – To see the endgame of no fear, please ask your humanness to be expanded to a state of Divine, in trust with no more fear. Ask the Plurality for your Highest Good to be of service to that endgame.

MASTER – Share the genius of light as a ritual of sharing, propulsion, and expansion. You are a pump of great consequence, radiating only trust.

PARTNER – Sometimes a recalibration of the relationship is needed. Clear open-ended time to go through all the categories still gnawing in need of transmutation to trust with no more fear.

DATE _____

PLACE _____

TIME _____

WHAT IS MINE TO DO?

Ask the expansive part of yourself.

_____

_____

WHAT IS MINE TO KNOW OR UNDERSTAND THAT I WOULDN'T EVEN KNOW TO ASK?

You are asking your Highest Self to be open to that which you may never have imagined. You are asking to see beyond your customary beliefs, ideas, and construction. Leave room for the possibility of receiving answers in both conventional and unconventional ways.

HOW CAN I LOVE MYSELF BEST RIGHT NOW?

As if you are listening to a friend, stay empty, feel, see, hear, know. If it's more comfortable, close your eyes to receive. Then write whatever comes to you—with no judgment or editing. If you are visual and images come, write what you see. If you hear an internal voice, small or large, write what you hear. If you have thoughts, body sensations, or emotional knowing, take notes. You are chronicling your expansion, a wondrous winding road, a treasure that is all yours.

41

The Wonder

*J*UST AS WE COME TOGETHER, we also serve the distance of perception. There are enough lotus blossoms of transformation to render the beauty of unfolding.

We come as a unified understanding. We rest easy in the arms of the other. There are no appointed results to justify the distance of perceptions. We are the many who are ready to see. We are the connected and affected who wish to lull the conscious to a surrendered attitude of want. Here we go and see it as the wonder.

We cannot wait to reveal the multidimensional efforts that exist. We take from the well of life and see the expression as deeper and more profound than ever before. We are waking up to understand the hope and life that springs eternal.

You make the life you live by the construction of your thoughts and actions.

You make the life you live to suggest you are connected.

As a stone enters the stream, a rush of water surrounds the newly submerged weight, but the stone itself has meaning in the entry. You make meaning in the life you express, and the meaning itself is also part of the expression. Your heart is also a contribution. Unseen, intangible movements such as love, feelings, and thoughts make up the life you express. Also the effects of your physics are at the reach of the collective feeling, thinking, and loving you in return.

Breaks are needed to short-circuit the reactions and impressions. Listen carefully to yourself. Listen carefully to nature. Listen with care and concern to the efforts of the other. Start to "go in" on all that rests near your head and limbs.

Start to whisper the song that is closest to your heart. You are now of the quantum, and you express through gossamer dimensions that hush in whispers and wing in wisps of visions and love.

See the many that surround your being and make them your friends. They are a wondrous extension of your expression. There is a consciousness that expresses on your behalf at a moment's notice to allow you the support of creation itself.

EXERCISE 41: GO IN

Take a nature walk. Commune with all that surrounds you: water, sky, trees, flowers, snow, green meadows, grass, rocks, mountains.

To "go in" is similar to bi-locating, just that we are now conversing with nature.

What is it that you want to tell me?

What are the feelings I feel for and from you?

(Scan your body, your thoughts, and your feelings and connect with all that is around you; even the wind is filled with consciousness.)

How does nature want to support me?

How can I serve nature back?

May I make a special prayer to stay open to the wonder of all that connects to me?

What is the meaning of the entry of my being into the greatness of nature?

Induction to Meditation

Please see page xvii.

Personalize Your Practice

BEGINNER – Our energies are very different from the plant kingdom's. The plant kingdom's are more refined.

Slow your breaths. Enter energetically and merge with the top of the tree where the photosynthesis and symbiosis is most active. See if you feel, think, and understand more than a moment before you entered.

MASTER – Air, wind, and breath all have consciousness. Ask the less dense consciousness of air if it has anything to share. Thank it for its support. Love this world you are gifted as a dense being in representation and growth of all the soul-consciousness in support of your physical self.

PARTNER – As we have deceased ancestors who come to our support for our life in life, so too do the plant and animal kingdoms. Talk to the consciousness of your symbiotic neighbors and thank them for their partnership. We are a symbiotic ecosystem of life in life and love in love.

DATE

PLACE

TIME

WHAT IS MINE TO DO?

Ask the expansive part of yourself.

WHAT IS MINE TO KNOW OR UNDERSTAND THAT I WOULDN'T EVEN KNOW TO ASK?

You are asking your Highest Self to be open to that which you may never have imagined. You are asking to see beyond your customary beliefs, ideas, and construction. Leave room for the possibility of receiving answers in both conventional and unconventional ways.

HOW CAN I LOVE MYSELF BEST RIGHT NOW?

As if you are listening to a friend, stay empty, feel, see, hear, know. If it's more comfortable, close your eyes to receive. Then write whatever comes to you—with no judgment or editing. If you are visual and images come, write what you see. If you hear an internal voice, small or large, write what you hear. If you have thoughts, body sensations, or emotional knowing, take notes. You are chronicling your expansion, a wondrous winding road, a treasure that is all yours.

42

Rules of the Road

DEAR ONES,
Here are the rules of the road.

1. Always see the other as yourself.
2. Never justify the best results as yours and yours alone.
3. Remember that there are times when we lose.
4. Reach out for neighbors, friends, and loved ones.
5. Don't help yourself alone; helping, regard, and lifting is for the whole at large.
6. Reach for the stars; aim high and let it all unfold.
7. Reach down, too; lift for others less fortunate.
8. Remember to ask not what you can do; ask what you are.
9. Living out loud can cause reverberations of great result; do not hide or underutilize; do not dim your light, your gifts.
10. Instead of living an Earthly existence, keep your head and heart open for a multidimensional existence.

EXERCISE 42: WHOLE AT LARGE

Who am I? (Feel into your vastness as you ask.)
  What am I? (Feel into your unity to the all as you inquire.)

Induction to Meditation

Please see page xvii.

Personalize Your Practice

BEGINNER – Knowing just who you are on all fronts is a beautiful opening that few have endeavored to ask. Just in the asking is the potential for answers beyond your wildest imagination. Stay open, inquire, and trust.

MASTER – Ask, "Who am I?" In respect to the vast express you are to yourself and to many, see yourself as the front man of a battalion of ancients, masters, and ancestors behind you. Your legacy is a gift of support from behind with many assisting from many different aspects of you. Bask in the glory of your being from the multitude behind you as well as the multitudes you touch. (Even if on the etheric planes of dreams, wonderings, and travel, your energy touches many.)

PARTNER – See who you are to each other, beyond the exercise. See if you can approach all facets of the way you interconnect and exist, each to each, as one to one. See—truly see—yourself as each other, as same and united.

DATE _____

PLACE _____

TIME _____

WHAT IS MINE TO DO?

Ask the expansive part of yourself.

_____

_____

_____

_____

WHAT IS MINE TO KNOW OR UNDERSTAND THAT I WOULDN'T EVEN KNOW TO ASK?

You are asking your Highest Self to be open to that which you may never have imagined. You are asking to see beyond your customary beliefs, ideas, and construction. Leave room for the possibility of receiving answers in both conventional and unconventional ways.

_____

_____

_____

_____

_____

HOW CAN I LOVE MYSELF BEST RIGHT NOW?

As if you are listening to a friend, stay empty, feel, see, hear, know. If it's more comfortable, close your eyes to receive. Then write whatever comes to you—with no judgment or editing. If you are visual and images come, write what you see. If you hear an internal voice, small or large, write what you hear. If you have thoughts, body sensations, or emotional knowing, take notes. You are chronicling your expansion, a wondrous winding road, a treasure that is all yours.

43

Call On Us

THERE ARE MANY of you who cannot see the horizon of love and light. Caught up in worry and malice, you have become victims of fear-based reactions. We can get you out of the loop. Please call on us, whatever your belief system.

Call on us. We are your ancestors, your angels, God, saints, masters, universal energies, and the love of mankind and nature. We are anything you can name that is used for your higher cause. Please do not hesitate to call. We are really here.

Just as you are in a loop, so are we ready and able to help release the patterns of your thinking and feeling and reactions. You are a wondrous being that can reach the limits of what you dream. Let go of the old and get ready for the bounty ready to be expressed.

Open your arms and let it all in. Lift them up high, listen to the words of Jesus: "Regard all," and "Judge not lest you be judged."

We make up the many, and the energies are very potent. They help you understand, regard, enlist your life's dreams.

Reap the rewards of the dreams that will take you aboard the ship of freedom.

Loops are of no use. Dare to dream. Dare to ask for help, even from the highest parts of your self.

There is a light at the end of the tunnel. Here it is and we are all one.

EXERCISE 43: LOOPS ARE OF NO USE

What loops in my thinking, feeling, and body reactions need to be readdressed?

Where do I judge myself still?

I call on all that is sacred and holy to me to bring me more clarity, assistance, the ability to love myself/others and to fulfill dreams. Please speak.

Induction to Meditation

Please see page xvii.

Personalize Your Practice

BEGINNER – Looping and perseverations are often programmed brain patterns that can be rewired. The act of meditation—slowing the breaths, calling on support from awe that is bigger than your own sense of self, prayer, or active renunciation of the old from a high vibration—will de-wire the loop cycle. Stay trusting that that day will come. Fervent ritual of new, positive transmutation will de-wire looping so that trust will replace old thought patterns. Remember to forgive the old thinking, find the positive aspects of you that also came from that source, and neutralize its existence. For all is *for* you, not done *to* you. Even if you were a victim, it is your job now to make lemonade from the lemons. You are a high being ready to transmute darkness to light.

MASTER – Hard as it is, scrutinize, inventory, and/or scour all parts of you that you may still hold in judgment.

PARTNER – Sometimes our partner/partners can see areas where we might still judge ourselves. Please, with kindness and from a loving place, inquire from your Highest Self just how to phrase the offering you are about to make to your partner for their benefit. Remember to ask from your Highest Self for two reasons: 1) not to disturb your partner's timing, as their readiness to receive the offering may not be there; and 2) to be aware of what is yours to do and why.

DATE

PLACE

TIME

WHAT IS MINE TO DO?

Ask the expansive part of yourself.

WHAT IS MINE TO KNOW OR UNDERSTAND THAT I WOULDN'T EVEN KNOW TO ASK?

You are asking your most high self to be open to that which you may never have imagined. You are asking to see beyond your customary beliefs, ideas, and construction. Leave room for the possibility of receiving answers in both conventional and unconventional ways.

_____

_____

_____

_____

_____

HOW CAN I LOVE MYSELF BEST RIGHT NOW?

As if you are listening to a friend, stay empty, feel, see, hear, know. If it's more comfortable, close your eyes to receive. Then write whatever comes to you—with no judgment or editing. If you are visual and images come, write what you see. If you hear an internal voice, a small or large voice, write what you hear. If you have thoughts, body sensations, or emotional knowing, take notes. You are chronicling your expansion, a wondrous winding road, a treasure that is all yours.

_____

_____

_____

_____

_____

_____

_____

44

Unveil a Layer of Perception

*H*OW SIMPLE IT IS to foretell of a time when you will unveil a layer of perception to worlds unexperienced before.

You are about to enter a zone of perception that will rip apart the fabric of your reality.

Please understand that each increment of revision and exploration will render results that oppose all that your well-meaning caregivers have imposed.

Each generation of this reality has lusted for understanding and simplicity.

Although one might, after knowledge is exposed, feel that we were making it more difficult, we were well-meaning in our collusions to experience this one reality with importance to all the rest.

Humans are in an agreed-upon perception that this dense, linear reality is the predominant expression. That is not the case.

Your consciousness plays outside your body multiple times per day and throughout your life. Much consciousness enters your physical being while you are in the day-to-day perceptions.

We are indeed all one.

The Divine is a summation of the all. All that we have expressed. All that we are to express and all that is. The all is comprised of each and every expression. It is a vast nod to the all, as it springs from all that is in every dimension and every formation.

The dense reality of previously fear-based construction was necessary to render us unaware of our newer expansion. Thus, perceptions based in fear rewarded linear thinking.

In Bali, children are taught to fear the sea gods. Understandably so, as tsunamis are an occasional occurrence. That fear serves to keep the children, when they become adults, from leaving the island. It keeps them from not exploring alternate realms. So, too, our fear-based resistance to expansion, to face the unknown, leaves us mired in the muck of one shared reality that no longer serves the widening expanse we are unanimously clamoring for.

Raise your heads to the heavens and request from above the opening results of your new expansion. No longer do we need fear to grow. We are now entering a zone of reveal. Slowly, slowly, we all jump aboard a moving ribbon of reveal to attain great experience of enlightenment.

EXERCISE 44: ENTERING A ZONE OF REVEAL

Pledging to not be distracted by Earthly chronology, extinguishing the need for past, present, and future or linear result, I implore all that is holy and sacred unto me to reveal. Please speak. (Write in stream of consciousness that which flows.)

Induction to Meditation

Please see page xvii.

Personalize Your Practice

BEGINNER – Open the aperture of your previous ways and means of perception to begin a new adventure in seeing all that is connected for you, to you, and of you. Even though it may not appear right away, begin the seeing with new understanding. Start connecting the dots differently. Make sense differently. This exercise requires uninterrupted time and sacred surroundings. You are about to enlarge your perceptions without causing backlash to your world. You now have enough foundation to be readied and primed. Trust in what you receive.

MASTER – Ask to be given newer additions of perception than anything ever received before. You are ready for maximum expansion. Alternate realms of you and beyond are here to assist.

PARTNER – Ask that your partnership be revealed as to all the realms on which it plays out. You are ready for the expansion and reveal. Stay clear, bright, and in trust.

DATE _____

PLACE _____

TIME _____

WHAT IS MINE TO DO?

Ask the expansive part of yourself.

_____

_____

_____

_____

_____

WHAT IS MINE TO KNOW OR UNDERSTAND THAT I WOULDN'T EVEN KNOW TO ASK?

You are asking your Highest Self to be open to that which you may never have imagined. You are asking to see beyond your customary beliefs, ideas, and construction. Leave room for the possibility of receiving answers in both conventional and unconventional ways.

_____

_____

_____

_____

_____

HOW CAN I LOVE MYSELF BEST RIGHT NOW?

As if you are listening to a friend, stay empty, feel, see, hear, know. If it's more comfortable, close your eyes to receive. Then write whatever comes to you—with no judgment or editing. If you are visual and images come, write what you see. If you hear an internal voice, small or large, write what you hear. If you have thoughts, body sensations, or emotional knowing, take notes. You are chronicling your expansion, a wondrous winding road, a treasure that is all yours.

45

Enlightenment

ALL EXPRESSION IS VALID.

What if the opening to alternate consciousness, not just your defined and discrete states, is opposing that which is not discernible to the eyes, ears, nose, or exterior body?

We are here to give such an opportunity to those who want such an opening.

But what occurs when there is opposition and revolt? Aha!

The fears that arise when one is attracted to fear-based energies inform just a small quadrant of experience. Yet when we are open to join with the light, face the darker parts of our own nature, and surrender to the all, we can be brothers and sisters and children to a greater gift of light and love.

We are here to make sure there is a testimonial of alignment/ adjustment. Those will come forward to experience that which they have never experienced before. Together we can, through love of self and other at the same time, not only see all the unique expressions of expansion, but also share in each other's burgeoning light.

We are the all.

EXERCISE 45: TESTIMONIAL OF ADJUSTMENT

Sit in the feeling of self-worth. Know that all your life, *all your life*, has brought you to this moment. Sit in that time line. Make a mental, emotional, and physical time line of your life and see, feel, and know the gorgeousness of you.

Induction to Meditation

Please see page xvii.

Personalize Your Practice

BEGINNER – The opposition might be alternate realms, energies, consciousness that follows you home from work and enters your body or personal field. Ask it to leave, directly. You want only to be of and surrounded by that which is of the highest qualities of love and light, the genius of love and light.

The reason we do this over and over again is that, as you become a beacon of the light, a light-worker, more riffraff is attracted to you.

MASTER – Transmutation of the opposing energies, realms, and consciousness is more active as you expand your being and reach higher and higher vibrations. Let an emissary such as Archangel Michael, Prophet Mohammed, Ganesh, Buddha Consciousness, or Creator help. Let them offer invitation to the energies for enlightenment. Often the dark is just uninterpreted light, waiting for illumination and invitation for expansion.

PARTNER – Enlightenment is, yes, your knowing that you are connected to all that ever was, is, and will be, but also reverence for the connection to self and other at the same time. Openhearted sharing is needed now. Ask to be vulnerable enough, courageous enough, to share all that has never been shared before, yet needs to be known. Have the sharing come after you have both entered each other's hearts' space.

DATE _____

PLACE _____

TIME _____

WHAT IS MINE TO DO?

Ask the expansive part of yourself.

_____

_____

_____

_____

_____

_____

WHAT IS MINE TO KNOW OR UNDERSTAND THAT I WOULDN'T EVEN KNOW TO ASK?

You are asking your Highest Self to be open to that which you may never have imagined. You are asking to see beyond your customary beliefs, ideas,

and construction. Leave room for the possibility of receiving answers in both conventional and unconventional ways.

HOW CAN I LOVE MYSELF BEST RIGHT NOW?

As if you are listening to a friend, stay empty, feel, see, hear, know. If it's more comfortable, close your eyes to receive. Then write whatever comes to you—with no judgment or editing. If you are visual and images come, write what you see. If you hear an internal voice, small or large, write what you hear. If you have thoughts, body sensations, or emotional knowing, take notes. You are chronicling your expansion, a wondrous winding road, a treasure that is all yours.

46

Monumental

*T*HIS IS A MONUMENTAL occurrence of phenomenal proportion that will affect the many and the few.

We are here in a fabulous time that affords all great loving energies to flow through our planet and the many.

Just as you have felt flushes of love for self and others at moments in your life, just as you have learned to love in moments of your life, it all is here!

Rejoice for the occurrence, as many have prayed for this moment. We are all in connection to the greatest good that this energetic connection can provide.

Here we are assigning meaning to the time when it will occur, and it is here!

Yes, time is a construction of mass agreement.

EXERCISE 46: MASS AGREEMENT

I have prayed many times in my life for this moment and it is here. Let me feel all the worlds fill me with love.

What mass agreements have now been made to feel and be of this love?

Induction to Meditation

Please see page xvii.

Personalize Your Practice

BEGINNER – The doing and redoing of prayers is to ritualize gratitude and the evolution of our spiritual revolution. Each time you are in gratitude to self and others at the same time, you raise your/the vibration to new heights. Your integration to deeper and richer understanding catapults life in life to new expression of grace and glory. Keep your Light Worker shining!

MASTER – Trust that the exact time you read this chapter will be the exact time for you to receive its message. This book is your living testament to your evolution. Even if you flip open pages with seeming abandon in a random style, know that that is never the case. All is here just for you, in perfect timing to your reception. Life in life is with you, for you, of you, and propelling you toward your greatest expansion of expression in every act of self-love.

PARTNER – Ask your partner again if any new agreements have been made and not consciously shared. See if your union's contract includes complete open regard for no editing, or are some agreements never to be spoken? Agree to the pact after mutuality is congruent to the love you have for one another. In each reflection, both of you are different and anew. Reviewing and agreeing on improvements is the way of the Positive System. We grow best through connection, collaboration, improvisation, co-creation, and humor. All is on track.

DATE _____

PLACE _____

TIME _____

WHAT IS MINE TO DO?

Ask the expansive part of yourself.

_____

_____

_____

_____

_____

WHAT IS MINE TO KNOW OR UNDERSTAND THAT I WOULDN'T EVEN KNOW TO ASK?

You are asking your Highest Self to be open to that which you may never have imagined. You are asking to see beyond your customary beliefs, ideas, and construction. Leave room for the possibility of receiving answers in both conventional and unconventional ways.

_____

_____

_____

_____

_____

HOW CAN I LOVE MYSELF BEST RIGHT NOW?

As if you are listening to a friend, stay empty, feel, see, hear, know. If it's more comfortable, close your eyes to receive. Then write whatever comes to you—with no judgment or editing. If you are visual and images come, write what you see. If you hear an internal voice, small or large, write what you hear. If you have thoughts, body sensations, or emotional knowing, take notes. You are chronicling your expansion, a wondrous winding road, a treasure that is all yours.

47

Mass Purpose

HERE WE ARE after the expression of "connected love." Just as we are in the expression of clarity for our unique purpose, we are also here for the collective understanding of timely purpose together.

This understanding is of great magnitude. We hopefully regret for nothing, we lust for nothing, and we want for nothing.

As we express together, we become harmonic of one and list ourselves as a very beautiful retreat of unison. We repeat old patterns but with a newness of intention and purpose. We are here. We are here.

Joy is our course. Love is our means. Regrets are for no one, as we are all one. Loops are an experience of sameness that will unite repetitive openings to new explorations. Listen for the new harmonic of love and connection. We are one. Repeat nothing. Find the new in all.

EXERCISE 47: FIND THE NEW IN ALL

Imagine your loops as round-and-round motions that need to be intervened upon. Take an imaginary feather and sever the loop's ring of motion. Rejoice as you also imagine the new motion of the loop as two arms that embrace you. Feel the love of the oneness.

Meditate on the last phrase: "We are one. Repeat nothing. Find new in the all." Write about it.

Induction to Meditation

Please see page xvii.

Personalize Your Practice

> **BEGINNER** – "Find new in the all" is a meditation for life lived in unity to the perfection of everything. Live your life as a prayer of love of self and others at all times. Even if dastardly events befall, see the growth from each occurrence as a gift of life in a body. Experience all of life's palate with the joy that it is your life, not be squandered but to be enjoyed for every last drop of expression for, in, and of your expansion!

> **MASTER** – Your own self-guided imaginings, ponderings, and feelings are of the quintessential expanse of your vast glory. Shoot high, dream big, and manifest!

> **PARTNER** - Imagine, ponder, or feel those interventions that might be best for today's coming together, as today holds the assistance to all that the union needs.

DATE _____

PLACE _____

TIME _____

WHAT IS MINE TO DO?

Ask the expansive part of yourself.

_____

_____

_____

_____

_____

WHAT IS MINE TO KNOW OR UNDERSTAND THAT I WOULDN'T EVEN KNOW TO ASK?

You are asking your Highest Self to be open to that which you may never have imagined. You are asking to see beyond your customary beliefs, ideas, and construction. Leave room for the possibility of receiving answers in both conventional and unconventional ways.

_____

_____

_____

_____

_____

HOW CAN I LOVE MYSELF BEST RIGHT NOW?

As if you are listening to a friend, stay empty, feel, see, hear, know. If it's more comfortable, close your eyes to receive. Then write whatever comes to you—with no judgment or editing. If you are visual and images come, write what you see. If you hear an internal voice, small or large, write what you hear. If you have thoughts, body sensations, or emotional knowing, take notes. You are chronicling your expansion, a wondrous winding road, a treasure that is all yours.

48

All Is Divine—Template for the Other Side

WHO IS TO UNDERSTAND when there is so much to be given? We cannot even fathom the permutations of life here on Earth. But request has been made and there is so much to explain.

First, there are no unforeseen circumstances; all is Divine.

Those from the other side who tell you otherwise are still in denial as to the meaning of their life and the impact they fail to resist seeing. They have dedicated their life on Earth as a symbol of regret, remorse, resistance, and worship. As we are all one, we are them and they are us. They help us open to begin to fathom.

When invested in acts of love, there is nothing more than Divine.

We resist as failure to truly see the enormity of the all and its connection.

We are one big soul. Everyone and everything is Divine, whether you can truly see it or not.

Here are the templates of the other side:

- ✍ Never denounce anything or anyone.
- ✍ Always see the bright side: the glass half full, the Divine in everything, silver lining, lemons into lemonade, and so on.

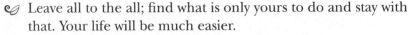

- Leave all to the all; find what is only yours to do and stay with that. Your life will be much easier.
- Hold no bars. Let down defenses, as we are all one.
- Justify nothing. Feel only what we are: a unit of experience to create, co-create, improvise, and feel.
- Realize, manifest, and complete as quickly as you can imagine. Parallel realities and alternate universes are created in just an instant; therefore creation is marvelous and rich.
- Listen to the footsteps of those before you. They are here whether they reincarnated, took alternate direction, or not. They have much to teach. There are places to reach the pockets of their imprint: graveside is best, as their dense remains still hold the impressions of their lives.
- Jump to conclusions and we have lost the very essence and gist of this life: experience and express.

These are the rules, the guidelines of our side... You get to make yours. Some are very tired of conflict, resistance, and revolt. In order for your dense expression to unfold with more order and loving here, please review our codes and see if we can teach you a newer way to relate.

Be worthy of your body and never give it a second thought; give it a first thought, as it is your vehicle to be.

We have made this clear to many who live it daily. See it in their laugh and smile and grace. Then, if that fits, take it on, for the many yearning for experience in a new way can still be of the dense world and enjoy the gifts of you as one in Divine smooth accordance to love and light, with all being of love and light, no matter what.

EXERCISE 48: LIVE IT DAILY

Write a prayer for you to fathom the all.

Induction to Meditation

Please see page xvii.

Personalize Your Practice

BEGINNER – "Those from the other side who tell you otherwise are still in denial as to the meaning of their life and the impact they fail to resist seeing." This means that if your guidance ever feels or communicates anything but positive, supportive, nonjudgmental words or uplifting bodily feelings while in meditation, then it is possible that some of your guidance that has not yet "gone to the light" is infiltrating your meditations. Only that which is of the highest qualities of the supreme genius of love and light, that which is here for your Highest Good, is invited in to your meditation.

"Going to the light" is a choice to attend a life review school that is entered upon dropping one's physical form. Sometimes those who have had a near-death experience or other spiritually transformative experience may also have had an earthbound knowing of that school. A consciousness chooses that school to reconcile their life. That school has different names and expressions in many different belief systems, but the light remains consistent.

Only have elevated feelings and knowings in an upholding of love and light, however you define it, while meditating and while in day-to-day life. You are of love all ways, always.

MASTER – See if your daily life holds the same truths as the template for the guidance realm. The templates may very well be the same. You are then refined in energy, elevated in heart, and in the perpetual kiss between heaven and earth. You are the angel you knew yourself to be. We love you always, forever and beyond.

PARTNER – Write a prayer for you to fathom the all, and share it with your partner. Read it aloud. Be of openhearted, undefended grace. You are a vast being of light and love all ways, always. We love you.

DATE

PLACE

TIME

WHAT IS MINE TO DO?

Ask the expansive part of yourself.

WHAT IS MINE TO KNOW OR UNDERSTAND THAT I WOULDN'T EVEN KNOW TO ASK?

You are asking your Highest Self to be open to that which you may never have imagined. You are asking to see beyond your customary beliefs, ideas, and construction. Leave room for the possibility of receiving answers in both conventional and unconventional ways.

_____

_____

_____

_____

HOW CAN I LOVE MYSELF BEST RIGHT NOW?

As if you are listening to a friend, stay empty, feel, see, hear, know. If it's more comfortable, close your eyes to receive. Then write whatever comes to you—with no judgment or editing. If you are visual and images come, write what you see. If you hear an internal voice, small or large, write what you hear. If you have thoughts, body sensations, or emotional knowing, take notes. You are chronicling your expansion, a wondrous winding road, a treasure that is all yours.

_____

_____

_____

_____

_____

_____

_____

_____

_____

49

No Turning Back

HERE WE ARE, and there is no turning back.

Just as the moment we were born into existence, now again there are unforeseen circumstances that allow us to recreate our newest designs of life. Here we are anew in the field of expression and existence.

Overnight everyone signed on to the results requested. Everyone and everything alive is now, with effort, resisting the impressions of their forefathers and allowing the newest openings. Widely accepted understanding is here.

We are to understand the greatest opening of our time: Brother will love brother; mother will love children. Each experience of expression will contain love in the new without regard solely for self. Love of self and other at the same time.

EXERCISE 49: YOUR PRAYERS

What is my personal prayer for today? (Consider writing one for yourself every day.)

Induction to Meditation

Please see page xvii.

Personalize Your Practice

BEGINNER – Each day there is revision and co-creation for your life, your soul, your body's rejuvenation ability. This is a time to boldly revise anything needing review. This may be an arena you have never meditated on before. Stay open in trust. All is here for you.

MASTER – You are divinely directed, protected, and connected. Your personal prayer is the path of today's co-creation. Enjoy the bounty.

PARTNER – Let's open up partnering to other realms in writing and sharing your personal prayer. See if any consciousness for your Highest Good wants to share from alternate realms the gifts of love and light they have for you, this day and every day.

DATE _____

PLACE _____

TIME _____

WHAT IS MINE TO DO?

Ask the expansive part of yourself.

_____

_____

_____

_____

_____

WHAT IS MINE TO KNOW OR UNDERSTAND THAT I WOULDN'T EVEN KNOW TO ASK?

You are asking your Highest Self to be open to that which you may never have imagined. You are asking to see beyond your customary beliefs, ideas, and construction. Leave room for the possibility of receiving answers in both conventional and unconventional ways.

_____

_____

_____

_____

_____

HOW CAN I LOVE MYSELF BEST RIGHT NOW?

As if you are listening to a friend, stay empty, feel, see, hear, know. If it's more comfortable, close your eyes to receive. Then write whatever comes to you—with no judgment or editing. If you are visual and images come, write what you see. If you hear an internal voice, small or large, write what you hear. If you have thoughts, body sensations, or emotional knowing, take notes. You are chronicling your expansion, a wondrous winding road, a treasure that is all yours.

50

They Serve the Many

THERE ARE MANY who choose to be here. They understand that it is theirs to do. Much like soldiers who put themselves in harm's way to protect their country, family, and group, these souls come through the portal of birth to announce a new change in direction. They serve the many who want expansion and betterment.

Realizing that they are in pain is the most difficult awakening. There is no fear at first; that takes time. At first our evolution is our devolution from the consciousness of "one."

We take on our individuality to perform in the illusion of separate. We exist to experience and express. We understand that each small increment of experience away from fear is the way we must now evolve.

Only then are we in the reverie of the all and our version of God. Join the group and see yourself as one, and you remedy the place you hold within the all.

There are no holds barred, and we unite to join a holy union to love of self and other at the same time. We expand consciousness to include all that exists, and we experience ourselves in holy matrimony with the Divine.

This expanded experience opens the all to once again repair the fear, deficit, chaos, and confusion. Persons of flesh expression will no longer require evidence to prove their connections to multi-dimensions. Persons can exist free to experience joy and completion with ease, trust, peace, and deep expressions of love.

Leave the rest to us. As a guiding force of consciousness, we assist in helping all to know what is theirs to do in every moment. There will be crooked lines to effectuate experiences that are not telegraphed in every moment. To learn and grow, one must not know all that will transpire. There is always growth to make expansion fun.

All consciousness is mutable and exchangeable. This is nothing to fear. Actually, you have done it for your entire lifetime, and you continue in the etheric expressions as well. We assist each other.

One might join into your body to warn you of possible danger or threat. Several might join you to assist in "filling you in." Electromagnetic fields, wave fields, and particle fields come to assist in healing or direction or course correction. We are divinely protected, directed, and connected at all times.

Even those who do not believe come to take part. Their conscious understanding is such to "denounce," but it persists in acting as the structure for resistance and rebellion, necessary to experience for many. They help the many to believe in direct experience, while they experience indirectly.

Listen to the soft or expletive phrases that have permeated speech of all languages, and see the ways of our realm in yours. We are one. Whether you pray, reflect, scream, or ask for help from silence within, we are here to give you assistance. We are one. We are you. We are able to exist for you, with you, of you, no matter where you are. We cross-sect dimensions and time as we conceive them.

We are the omniscient all that exists for the all. There is no death, only reference from alternate, primary expression.

You have the gift to be able to do what we do. You work very hard on the dream plane, in prayers, and in pointed energetic request.

There is nothing that cannot be accomplished. If we dream and imagine, then it is done. We are a sum of all that is and we can exist on multiple realms at all times.

Join in knowingly; there is less resistance, refusal, and rebellion. Join in consciously and feel the ability to express and experience without the existential angst that comes with feeling alone.

You are never alone, but you must know how to ask for help. The very act of asking strips one of perceived defenses that get in the way of helplessness, torturous emotions, and difficult internal states. Your body is a readout of the wear and tear of your life. Your experience of laughter, joy, humor, and freedom to be yourself is the freedom to be connected to all.

We need each other to find the humor and connect. We need each other to love more connectedly. We need each other to birth a baby into this world and repair the pain that has existed in that family line.

Soul groups, family groups, work groups, and play groups are all means to find the sense of collective joy and connection. Make them all count and call on that which serves your purpose and your way.

You are a gift of perception and connection, for the dense, physical flesh expression is not to be squandered. If we all came into awareness of how much mutual, shared, and accepted connection we exist with at all times, we would open awareness to our expanded self. We would no longer need to communicate and grow from resistance, rebellion, and repair.

We would elevate growth through the experience of love: improvisation, collaboration, co-creation, and connection. We would serve self and other at the same time. Honoring of self would be effortless. We would never feel the burden of "I." "I have to get this done." "I must not feel this way." All would understand that they are a "we" and would implore the "we" of the all to carefully assist in all matters consciously.

We would not only see more vividly the connection of the all to the self, but we would be attracting flesh expression groups that would be honoring our physical purpose as well.

We need not ask what is ours to do. After a while of living in expanded consciousness, it appears, it is apparent.

EXERCISE 50: INVITATION REQUIRED

Review all the ways the other side works:

- We serve the dense realm without its knowing.
- We knowingly serve each other together.
- We tag-team and keep the flow of exchange moving, but some of us are bound by location and evolution.
- Upon invitation in both directions, miracles happen when love, light, and clarity are included.

Loosen ideas around contemporary physics to include life in life. Join in and start the open invitation for miracles.

Write about all that you have experienced in concert to all realms. Offer invitation to the all for support.

Induction to Meditation

Please see page xvii.

Personalize Your Practice

BEGINNER – When you invite in miracles, expect that you just might *be* the miracle. Stay clear, bright, and steadfast in your trust. Try living consciously from the, in the, of the Positive System: co-create, cooperate, improvise, collaborate, connect. Try not to be in rebellion toward anything or anybody.

Check in with your Highest Self to assess what is yours to do.

MASTER – Work very assiduously at trying not to judge. Old parts of negative aspects of self rear up to be integrated. See them as a gift of growth. Ask how they have helped you, thank them for the good to date, and then let them expand into universal flow of the Positive System. It is a gift of compassion to self and other to still feel your humanness with forgiveness.

PARTNER – Sit silently touching in partner dyads. Stay with slowed breath, eyes closed, and feel the invitation of partner to partner for the miracle shared only by the two of you, in this moment, now. Give each other an agreed-upon amount of time to receive, and then share.

DATE

PLACE

TIME

WHAT IS MINE TO DO?

Ask the expansive part of yourself.

WHAT IS MINE TO KNOW OR UNDERSTAND THAT I WOULDN'T EVEN KNOW TO ASK?

You are asking your Highest Self to be open to that which you may never have imagined. You are asking to see beyond your customary beliefs, ideas, and construction. Leave room for the possibility of receiving answers in conventional and unconventional ways.

_____

_____

_____

_____

_____

HOW CAN I LOVE MYSELF BEST RIGHT NOW?

As if you are listening to a friend, stay empty, feel, see, hear, know. If it's more comfortable, close your eyes to receive. Then write whatever comes to you—with no judgment or editing. If you are visual and images come, write what you see. If you hear an internal voice, small or large, write what you hear. If you have thoughts, body sensations, or emotional knowing, take notes. You are chronicling your expansion, a wondrous winding road, a treasure that is all yours.

_____

_____

_____

_____

_____

51

Flesh Existence Is Service

WHILE YOU ALL AGREE to assign meaning to the flesh existence as a complete and sovereign effort, we cannot lift the veil. The best we can do is join you on the dream plane, when your corporeal body is asleep and your consciousness is roaming free.

There it is that you lift the veils and dare to work outside subscribed laws of dense reality with time.

Your body is earthbound in the way you have assigned meaning to grow. It is important to continue some of the laws of perception. You will rest easier in your body and relinquish doubts. While you are in daily wondering, we can open doors of perception, but please do not expect too much. That was the agreement before you took a body. (Drugs only widen the aperture, but they are by no means an accurate account of all that exists for you when you are not in your dense service.)

Remember you are of service in the flesh expression. You are not to avoid this realm as reasonable, although it is illusion. There are mass agreements that provide service for the grounding of our worlds. They are all one. They are you and you are us. We collide never. It is a concert, a dance of expressions in all realms, dimensions, and levels. We are all in the ethers.

We are all on other celestial bodies and space. You are vast in your expression. This is only a small remembrance as it is in action. Please notify yourself that as much as you would like to be of open regard for all that you are in all moments, it is impossible to traverse all expression in all realms within your body, a dense, mass-agreement reality.

However, once the mass agreement allows for a final frontier of expressions aligned in loving awareness, we can move the entirety away from dense direction. This would mean love of self and other at the same time. This is no small feat. Man and Earth consciousness have assigned meaning to beliefs that would need to be uprooted and replaced (e.g., "no pain, no gain," "when the road gets tough, the tough get going," "life would be boring if there was no struggle," "whatever does not kill me makes me stronger," etc.).

It is very different when one subscribes to "making lemonade out of lemons," or "God will never give me more than I can handle," as these aphorisms lend themselves to the positive experience of connection without fear.

Is man, in flesh experience, ready to denounce the very structures that he has formidably fought in the name of victory, growth, and survival? Will man want to accept that there is no death?

Is this the time that we can be called to elevate and expand our consciousness to grow from new experience? Can we assign import to "growth in the excitement of love," or "growth in the experience of love"? Only then can we dive into another expression of love of self and other at the same time. Only then must we be so open that we let each other in.

We bi-locate, we remote view, we begin new awareness that allows each of us to take down defenses. In the face of horror, we can have out-of-body experiences.

In the face of despair, we can have near-death experiences. These can be literal and figurative. There is much we can learn from using alternative parts of our being in flow with the all.

EXERCISE 51: PLEASE NOTIFY YOURSELF

Am I able to give up the mass agreement around survival as I have known it?

What idea of survival can include life in life and love of self and other at the same time?

Meditate, pray, reflect, ponder, and write. If you were in a state of wondering where the doors of perception flew open, what might your Highest Self be able to share?

Induction to Meditation

Please see page xvii.

Personalize Your Practice

BEGINNER – Your own sense of survival has been a foundation of life itself for so long. It is built into our DNA. How hard it will be to second-guess and reroute our perceived bedrock? But it is time. Fear is not the fuel of survival anymore.

MASTER – Ponder when the doors of perception flew open for you. How far back is your earliest memory of being touched by that which was beyond usual and customary? How long have you been silent? Is it time to share?

PARTNER – Discuss your writings with each other. This is a very difficult chapter, as it asks you to reconcile life in a body and life as eternal.

DATE _____

PLACE _____

TIME _____

WHAT IS MINE TO DO?

Ask the expansive part of yourself.

_____

_____

_____

_____

_____

WHAT IS MINE TO KNOW OR UNDERSTAND THAT I WOULDN'T EVEN KNOW TO ASK?

You are asking your Highest Self to be open to that which you may never have imagined. You are asking to see beyond your customary beliefs, ideas, and construction. Leave room for the possibility of receiving answers in both conventional and unconventional ways.

_____

_____

_____

_____

_____

HOW CAN I LOVE MYSELF BEST RIGHT NOW?

As if you are listening to a friend, stay empty, feel, see, hear, know. If it's more comfortable, close your eyes to receive. Then write whatever comes to you—with no judgment or editing. If you are visual and images come, write what you see. If you hear an internal voice, small or large, write what you hear. If you have thoughts, body sensations, or emotional knowing, take notes. You are chronicling your expansion, a wondrous winding road, a treasure that is all yours.

52

Leave All Reality to Illusion

*L*EAVE ALL REALITY to illusion, and then see if there is another informative foundation to express. See if all the ways and means by which we delineate the markings of structure melt into oblivion. See if all the constructs for the masses end up representing all that has been fooling us before and anon, as time is not linear.

Let us begin anew and see ourselves outside of time, out of relativity to all that we have conceived and perceived prior to the requests.

Now, if we imagine life experienced without constructs, are we then left alone or are we left with a divine sense of order?

Know that there are many who are relational to the all, and that is fine. Know that there are many who are relational to the all without knowing, and that is best for them. Know that there is in the works a new order of the nonsensical—not of the senses.

While we lust, yearn, or long for the meaning, we also get hamstrung by the very existence of structure laid upon judgments and constraints.

Here we go in releasing all deficits, confusion, chaos, and concerns. Here we go in forging new frontiers of laughter and love, devoid of illustrative fall-men and -women (people who take the brunt of the blame). Maybe now we can learn to take the heat when it really isn't hot. Maybe now we are ready to see that there is divine order in everything. There is nothing to want for and nothing to find.

Listen again the way we once knew. Listen from your heart where constructs are not present.

EXERCISE 52: LISTEN FROM YOUR HEART

Say out loud these demandments:

I accept and listen with an open heart.

I release the need to grow from deficit, confusion, chaos, and concern.

I release my mass agreement for constructs of limited; I accept my vastness.

I release my need for structures laden with judgment and constraint.

I accept humor as my primary embrace as I lovingly receive my connection to the all.

From my heart I accept that there is nothing to want for and nothing to find.

Induction to Meditation

Please see page xvii.

Personalize Your Practice

> **BEGINNER** – In saying these demandments out loud, you ritualize, concretize, ratify, and make holy your acceptance.

MASTER – Employ humor as a non-defense; laughter is enlightenment.

PARTNER – Look into each other's eyes as you say these words. Feel into the meaning for you as well as your partner. Share what came up for you as you spoke, as your partner spoke.

Check before you break connection, if you are indeed "complete" from this exercise.

Try to close with that extra beat of inquiry before breaking any connection. (Ask: "Are you complete? Am I complete? Are we complete?") Sometimes you feel done, but there is more on the table to share, process, or review. Take the extra closure moment to check in with each other.

DATE _____

PLACE _____

TIME _____

WHAT IS MINE TO DO?

Ask the expansive part of yourself.

_____

_____

_____

_____

_____

_____

WHAT IS MINE TO KNOW OR UNDERSTAND THAT I WOULDN'T EVEN KNOW TO ASK?

You are asking your Highest Self to be open to that which you may never have imagined. You are asking to see beyond your customary beliefs, ideas, and construction. Leave room for the possibility of receiving answers in both conventional and unconventional ways.

_____

_____

_____

_____

_____

HOW CAN I LOVE MYSELF BEST RIGHT NOW?

As if you are listening to a friend, stay empty, feel, see, hear, and know. If it's more comfortable, close your eyes to receive. Then write whatever comes to you—with no judgment or editing. If you are visual and images come, write what you see. If you hear an internal voice, small or large, write what you hear. If you have thoughts, body sensations, or emotional knowing, take notes. You are chronicling your expansion, a wondrous, winding road, a treasure that is all yours.

_____

_____

_____

_____

53

We Have Never Acted Alone

THERE IS NOTHING that will come between the person that you are and the results requested to expand further to the consciousness of the all. We are one. That being said, the reason we have an acceptance of body is to express universal betterment for the experience of the whole.

We do expect that over our lifetime we will have results to show that we are of our own making. Let us now stop to think of how we were always, all ways together with everyone, as no man creates himself in a vacuum.

We are now the product of shared cells as well as shared cosmic creation. We do nothing alone and have never done anything alone. We entreated a wish for alone to see ourselves as masters of a purposeful existence, but we have never acted alone.

EXERCISE 53: MASTERS OF A PURPOSEFUL EXISTENCE

Although I signed up for an experience of mastery toward a purposeful existence at a soul level, may I now in tandem, or in group, begin to feel my vastness with the all?

Induction to Meditation

Please see page xvii.

Personalize Your Practice

BEGINNER – This is a meditation that may bring a flood of information, feeling, and thoughts, or nothing at all. Trust that you are exactly where you need to be.

This is a book that can be done over and over again. As we grow and refine our sense of vastness, our intuitive information shifts too.

MASTER – Stay open for that which may have never spoken or connected to you before, to reach out. Stay empty to receive and feel; that which is to be heard will make itself known, but again, it must only be for your Highest Good.

PARTNER – Use this time to create an exercise of telepathy or intuition, as you have now been opened up. Always work with the understanding that all is for the Highest Good of both in mutuality for the expansion of the relationship.

DATE _____

PLACE _____

TIME _____

WHAT IS MINE TO DO?

Ask the expansive part of yourself.

_____

_____

_____

_____

_____

WHAT IS MINE TO KNOW OR UNDERSTAND THAT I WOULDN'T EVEN KNOW TO ASK?

You are asking your Highest Self to be open to that which you may never have imagined. You are asking to see beyond your customary beliefs, ideas, and construction. Leave room for the possibility of receiving answers in both conventional and unconventional ways.

_____

_____

_____

_____

_____

HOW CAN I LOVE MYSELF BEST RIGHT NOW?

As if you are listening to a friend, stay empty, feel, see, hear, know. If it's more comfortable, close your eyes to receive. Then write whatever comes to you—with no judgment or editing. If you are visual and images come, write what you see. If you hear an internal voice, small or large, write what you hear. If you have thoughts, body sensations, or emotional knowing, take notes. You are chronicling your expansion, a wondrous winding road, a treasure that is all yours.

54

Integrate All to the All

THE CONSCIOUSNESS that serves to negate and annihilate can serve no longer. We must go beyond that which serves the negative system to also include all consciousness not in service of love and light.

That which serves to negate is invited to be transmuted to positive, open, inclusive acceptance. That which serves to annihilate is invited to act as an agent of solidification toward understanding and light. All expression is valid.

That which is of consciousness with no service to love and light is invited to do so. We are here to integrate all to the all. We are here to allow for expansive reach in expression of all. With this invitation, I consecrate all that I am to be of love and light.

EXERCISE 54: HOW WE INTERPRET SERVES THE DARK

Highest Self, how might I co-create a new morality and construction for my life?

How might I now reinterpret difficulty to an agent of solidification toward understanding?

I invite all of my life to include open, positive acceptance for all interpretations. I will meditate on each conundrum as a new event toward revelation.

Induction to Meditation

Please see page xvii.

Personalize Your Practice

BEGINNER / MASTER / PARTNER – The completion of this go-round of the book is here! Success is yours!

Stay with the work. Use this book to illuminate reoccurring conundrums that arise. It is your working journal toward your expansion, and can be addressed over and over to find new, deeper layers of learning. The personality is an onion of new layers that reveal as we pull back top layers.

Your commitment to the Positive System is an antidote to the Polarity System. Regard all aspects of self as a balanced, symbiotic organism. If one piece of you needs attention then, most likely, another lynchpin, perhaps not yet known, may be at the causal root of that which is becoming newly seen, valued, and understood for integration, forgiveness, and appreciation in the Positive System.

Example: Gina needed to be rescued. Her setup was to be saved from those from her outside world. As she looked at how she was cutting herself off from her own power, she became aware that simultaneously she was in rebellion to a small faint voice trying to guide her from within.

She was in a setup of one-down in her physical world, having others reigning supreme in knowing, while playing one-up to her guidance. That seesaw of extremes is the Polarity System. One side of us fuels the other side. Both require each other for balance.

The Positive System is equanimity. No extreme. No seesaw. Trust and flow. The moment brings it all. We will grow from each moment of open wondering and reception to our expansion. The invitation to our most expanded and vast self is always on the table. The commitment to abide and listen to that which is from our Highest Self brings all. Remember forevermore: I AM LOVE.

When you are in mediation and elevated inquiry, over time, begin to address your new morality. Each question of ethics and personal choice is for only you to make, while in concert to the Highest Goodness of your vast beingness. Those private, still moments of reflection in the grace of your definition of the Divine is the gift of your life best lived in the privilege of this time on Mother Earth. You are always and forever in LIFE IN LIFE!

DATE

PLACE

TIME

WHAT IS MINE TO DO?

Ask the expansive part of yourself.

WHAT IS MINE TO KNOW OR UNDERSTAND THAT I WOULDN'T EVEN KNOW TO ASK?

You are asking your Highest Self to be open to that which you may never have imagined. You are asking to see beyond your customary beliefs, ideas,

and construction. Leave room for the possibility of receiving answers in both conventional and unconventional ways.

_____

_____

_____

_____

_____

_____

HOW CAN I LOVE MYSELF BEST RIGHT NOW?

As if you are listening to a friend, stay empty, feel, see, hear, know. If it's more comfortable, close your eyes to receive. Then write whatever comes to you—with no judgment or editing. If you are visual and images come, write what you see. If you hear an internal voice, small or large, write what you hear. If you have thoughts, body sensations, or emotional knowing, take notes. You are chronicling your expansion, a wondrous winding road, a treasure that is all yours.

_____

_____

_____

_____

AFTERWORD: All That You Are

IN COMPLETING this workbook, you are very unusual.

You have no idea who you are or what you have accomplished.

You want nothing. You only ask for worlds to accept and allow themselves to join in a higher octave of love. You live in perfect union.

You might preach, yes, but you ask of no one what you do not ask tenfold of yourself.

We are all, all here for YOU. You never have to doubt or wonder ever again.

You have a job that you are here to fulfill, now of your own making, as you have already completed what you were initially sent to do.

You took on your own divine nature to express without the dark—something no one thought possible of all consciousness. The etheric realms have signed on, the physical realms are thinking about it, but no matter, for if they decide to live of fear, they will eventually extinguish themselves. It is all on course.

You are to hear the chorus of loving beings in your corner. Worlds, dimensions, and all the universes have come together for your road of unity in acceptance and allowance, in love of self and other at the same time.

You make beauty wherever you go, because people see their own beauty from your eyes and love.

BONUS EXERCISES FOR PARTNERS:
Rules of Engagement for Couples

1. NO EDIT – Each person in the couple is invited to give voice to all of his or her innermost thoughts and feelings, no matter how rough or ill-formed, in order to cement a foundation of truth for the partnership. Nothing is out of bounds or too personal to share. However, all that is shared occurs after one or both take a beat and invite in universal consciousness of love and light to assist with the exchange.

2. ALL EXPRESSION IS VALID – There are positive lessons in even the most negative expression or the most trying events. If we are at all times connected in love through our guidance, then each member of a couple can stay open, allowing and accepting the other. There then exists the potential for understanding the less overt themes that may need to be uncovered and addressed.

3. BALANCE MASCULINE AND FEMININE – This is for both members of the couple, regardless of gender. With loving

regard, with calm and peace, we aspire to balance our masculine and feminine natures, not by controlling or doing or by playing submissive, victim, or martyr, but by being open to giving and receiving without negotiated exchange or pulling focus. Invite the other side to assist you in this process.

4. LOVE OF SELF AND OTHER AT THE SAME TIME – Because everyone is part of a collective and everything proceeds from an interconnected past, present, and future, neither partner in the couple needs to have dominion over the other. It is simply for you to love yourself and your partner at the same time. There is also no space for any blame, which is a backward step in projecting some failing within you or a blind spot or cover-up preventing you from calling on your Higher Self. Often we may "give" and lose our self in the process, or we "receive" and lose the other in the process. By inviting guidance and loving light, we make strides in taking our self and other in loving account at the same time.

5. GO FOR THE JOY – Your purpose is to enjoy life together. Co-create what will bring you both the most of what you want from your lives. Joy is what the two of you have decided to uphold for your expression as a coupleship. While in meditation, use your higher selves and your partnership with each other side to assist with your happiness here on earth. Often the guidance realm will supply a knowing to help you "know" what is yours to do.

6. MEDITATE & VOW – Write a relationship vow that you recite together every morning and evening while holding hands. Invite the universal consciousness of love and light to bring you guidance. In those moments, stay empty to hear what you can do today to better yourself, your relationship, and your world. Share your meditations. Honor each other, for in these moments you have consecrated your lives and your sacred union.

7. GIVE 110 PERCENT – When things begin going in a negative direction, or begin to spiral into a damage cycle, make a pact to sit down together, hold hands, and counsel with your higher selves and your guidance realm. Invoke the "no edit" rule, and stay free of judgment and blame. By interacting with another person with love and respect, we are also loving and respecting ourselves. By taking a beat to receive assistance from your guidance realm, you bring a higher perspective to a potentially devolving situation.

8. TRUST THAT ALL IS GUIDED AND ORCHESTRATED on behalf of the couple's goals. Revisit your vow and demandments. Write them as dynamic, fluid documents that can be revised. (Demandments are written directives to your guidance realm to deliver for your coupleship.)

9. SIT BACK AND LOVE – It is all effortless, because when you are engaged, alive, and passionate, the two of you are blessed with completion and ease.

EXERCISE: WRITE YOUR VOW

Meditate together on each section in Chapter 20, keeping notes. Institute the expression of your vow on a ritualized, sacred basis (such as before jumping out of bed in the morning or before going to sleep at night). Confer on all the rules. Try them on. Pick out together which pieces feel best to incorporate. Know that some of the rules may apply to other unions as well.

Induction to Meditation

Please see page xvii.

Personalize Your Practice

ROMANTIC PARTNERS – When you marry, marry on all realms, all dimensions, and all ways. Know that the new kind of love is a union with both of your Highest Selves operating from love of self and other at the same time, supported in grace.

PERSONAL AND/OR BUSINESS PARTNERS – You are not ever alone, as you are guided, connected, loved, and directed by your divine battalion of protection. For a personal vow and/or one for business partnerships, writing out your call to action will serve as guideposts for your life ahead.

DATE _____

PLACE _____

TIME _____

WHAT IS MINE TO DO?

Ask the expansive part of yourself.

_____

_____

_____

_____

_____

_____

WHAT IS MINE TO KNOW OR UNDERSTAND THAT I WOULDN'T EVEN KNOW TO ASK?

You are asking your Highest Self to be open to that which you may never have imagined. You are asking to see beyond your customary beliefs, ideas, and construction. Leave room for the possibility of receiving answers in both conventional and unconventional ways.

_____

_____

_____

_____

_____

HOW CAN I LOVE MYSELF BEST RIGHT NOW?

As if you are listening to a friend, stay empty, feel, see, hear, know. If it's more comfortable, close your eyes to receive. Then write whatever comes to you—with no judgment or editing. If you are visual and images come, write what you see. If you hear an internal voice, small or large, write what you hear. If you have thoughts, body sensations, or emotional knowing, take notes. You are chronicling your expansion, a wondrous winding road, a treasure that is all yours.

_____

_____

_____

_____

_____

The New Dyad Is Complete

JUST A WHILE AGO were great rumblings as to who you both were together. Now there is silence and refuge in the great knowing and feeling of love. Love without defense. Love internal and direct. Love in the state of unity.

When two people come together to love in partnership, they dissolve the need for defense.

This is a great day! Love of self and other is born from the wellspring of hope eternal, unity, and reasonable elimination of self and selflessness.

You are both ready to resume a life of whole—one and the same. There is a border, as thin membrane of vehicle, for the physical and for the distinction of what each provides in purpose and action, but the true essence of self/isness is complete. The union to unity and the union to each as an open regard for "we" and the same at the same time is complete!

Enjoy the days together and reap the rewards of your union to all and "we." *Carpe diem* means "seize the day" of this magnificence to revel in your accomplishments. Give honoring to the days leading up to this: speaking your truth, listening, and loving.

You both have earned the right to be married in physical, emotional, mental, and spiritual understanding. The bow is tied!

EXERCISE: STATE OF THE UNION

This is the chapter for those who have been working on their relationship together.

Although this is primarily a romantic love partnership, it can also be used for any partnership, as there is usually a physical component to many endeavors, even if not romantic in nature.

Having worked these steps together has brought each into a deeper knowing of self-love from an internal source of reference, and has brought each into a prospect of trying on the idea of dropping all defenses and joining with the universal consciousness of love.

In all three is the silence and refuge of great knowing and feeling of love.

Why, when I have love internal, can I release my need for defense and borders with you?

What are our distinct and unique purposes for the world and for each other?

What is the difference between selflessness/selfishness/self and other at the same time/self is-ness?

What might I never want to un-know about the state of my union to you (my partner) from before, and where are we now?

Induction to Meditation

Please see page xvii.

Personalize Your Practice

BEGINNER – Remember as you are both one, you are also discreet, sovereign in missions. You have purpose and missions that are separate, as individuals, and together, in relationship. Define both.

MASTER – Teach, show, and share with those around you why it is that in the silence, one understands self-love.

PARTNERS – If not romantic, the "physical component" means the mission of expression each soul has that impacts the world and each to each. Explore that.

DATE _____

PLACE _____

TIME _____

WHAT IS MINE TO DO?

Ask the expansive part of yourself.

_____

_____

_____

_____

_____

WHAT IS MINE TO KNOW OR UNDERSTAND THAT I WOULDN'T EVEN KNOW TO ASK??

You are asking your Highest Self to be open to that which you may never have imagined. You are asking to see beyond your customary beliefs, ideas, and construction. Leave room for the possibility of receiving answers in both conventional and unconventional ways.

HOW CAN I LOVE MYSELF BEST RIGHT NOW?

As if you are listening to a friend, stay empty, feel, see, hear, know. If it's more comfortable, close your eyes to receive. Then write whatever comes to you—with no judgment or editing. If you are visual and images come, write what you see. If you hear an internal voice, small or large, write what you hear. If you have thoughts, body sensations, or emotional knowing, take notes. You are chronicling your expansion, a wondrous winding road, a treasure that is all yours.

ABOUT THE AUTHOR

IN 1977, **DR. LEVIN** launched her career at what was to become Hollywood's premier talent agency, CAA. She was responsible for signing such celebrities as Michael Keaton, Madonna, and Michael Jackson. Then in 1985, she began her own film production company.

After almost 20 years in show business, she made the bold move to follow her true calling as a psychologist. Her breakthrough came as her mother was dying of cancer. With the recognition that death is simply a passageway to the next life, she helped her mother find peace in her transition. Dr. Levin was inspired to return to school to obtain her doctorate to explore new frontiers of health, wellness, and spirituality.

In 2004, Dr. Levin founded Moonview Sanctuary, a collaborative treatment and research institute created through the careful integration of modern psychology and neuroscience, together with ancient knowledge and spiritual practices from around the world.

In 2009, she published her award-winning memoir, *God, the Universe, and Where I Fit In*, illustrating her spiritual journey of transformation through intuition.

Dr. Levin and her husband, Jerry Levin, have recently co-founded The Levin Center for Parkinson's Transformational Health.

Visit:

laurieannlevin.com
moonviewsanctuary.com
thelevincenter.com